Saltian

"to dance"

Alice Shapiro

ISBN 978-1-936373-24-6

© 2012 Alice Shapiro. All rights reserved. No part of this publication may be reproduced or transmitted in any form or by any means, electronic or mechanical, without permission in writing from the publisher. Requests for permission to make copies of any part of this work should be e-mailed to info@unboundcontent.com.

Published in the United States by Unbound Content, LLC, Englewood, NJ.

Cover art: ©2012 Anne Hammel

Author photo: ©2012 John Barker

The poems in this collection are all original and previously unpublished with the exception of those credited otherwise.

Saltian

First edition 2012

Editorial Note

Welcome to an amazing editing adventure! The book you are reading is the result of a collaborative project undertaken by Alice Shapiro in the summer of 2011. She came to me with a simple, yet profound, question: how is a poem, a collection of poems, affected by another set of eyes?

To find out, we assembled a remarkable group of editors and writers to serve as the project's editorial board. Then we took Alice's poems and assigned them to the editorial board for critique. We posted each poem, critique, and even responsive art at unbound CONTENT's bookblog so that the reading public could weigh in. The posts are included here in an Appendix.

Alice went back and read each poem again with the critiques and public comments in mind. She revised the manuscript, sometimes making suggested changes, sometimes making no changes, sometimes making entirely different changes. The poems that make up the body of this collection are the final product of this interactive process. They can be read and enjoyed in their own right. They can be taught with the originals and critiques as part of a poetry study addressing the concept of editing and revising. They can be taken as part of a whole and read within the context of artistic evolution.

I am grateful to the editorial board for their enthusiastic and thoughtful participation and for the readers who responded so openly. I am honored to present this book to you and I hope you enjoy reading it as thoroughly as I have enjoyed publishing it.

—Annmarie Lockhart

Table of Contents

Introduction 13
Preface 17
Seven Mortal Steps 19

I. Infancy

Entrance 25
Where are you? 26
Look up at the green and blue 28
Grand Malia 29
INFANCY 30
End of the line 31
Infant, infant 32

II. Childhood

A cow woke me up 35
Why this, why that? 37
Miss K's arabesque 38
Dysfunction 39
The sea intrudes and calms 40
The Feast of St. Catherine 41
Seeds 42

III. Lover

In the morning, looking 45
Catching love 46
Where is the dance? 47
The transparency of a Spanish fly 48
Jealous plate 50
The salve of women meeting 51
Desire 52

IV. Soldier

A son's war 57
Not my war 58
Corporate war zones 59
Street wars 61
After war 63
Distant wars 64
Worst wars 65

V. The Justice

Laze away the day 69
The law of attraction 70
On walls 73
Rich man, poor man 74
Denial 75
Where is the justice in that? 76
Well done 77

VI. The Pantaloon, Old Age

Original face 81
Injustice 82
Photographs and sand 83
Not there yet 85
Second chances 86
Failing 88
Moving on 89

VII. Dementia and Death

Carey High School bleachers 93
Hell's kitchen 94
The strength of old ideals 95
Circles 96
Randomness near the end 97
Here and hereafter 98
Saltian 99

Postscript

A-head 102

Appendix. Original Poems With Critiques

Seven mortal steps 105
    Critique: Responsive writing, Robert CJ Graves 108
First entrance 109
    Critique, Ray Brown 109
Where are you? 110
    Critique, Lynne Thompson 111
Look up at the green and blue 114
    Critique, Bobbie Troy 115
Malia 116
    Critique, Carlene Tejada 117
I.N.F.A.N.C.Y. 118
    Critique, Andrew Badger 118
End of the line 120
    Critique, Joanie DiMartino 120
Infant, infant 122
    Critique, Leah Maines 122
A cow woke me up 124
    Critique, Walter Elmore 126
Why this, why that? 128
    Critique, Sarah Endo 128
Miss K's arabesque 130
    Critique, Grace Burns 131
Dysfunction 132
    Critique, Scott Owens 133
The sea intrudes and calms 135
    Critique, KC Bosch 136
The Feast of St. Catherine 137
    Critique: Responsive writing, Maxwell Baumbach 138
Sex 140
    Critique: Responsive writing, Bryan Borland 140

In the morning, looking	149
Critique, Joanna S Lee	149
Catching love	151
Critique, Ray Sharp	152
Where is the love?	154
Critique, Jim Valvis	155
The transparency of a Spanish fly	163
Critique, Stan Galloway	164
Jealous plate	167
Critique, Jean McLeod	168
The salve of women meeting	172
Critique: Responsive writing, KJ Hannah Greenberg	172
Desire	177
Critique, Harrison Solow	178
A son's war	181
Critique, Kenneth Karrer	181
Not my war	184
Critique, Kay Middleton	184
Corporate war zones	186
Critique, David B Axelrod	187
Street wars	189
Critique, Ray Brown	190
After war	192
Critique: Responsive writing, Bryan Borland	193
Critique: Responsive photo, Bryan Borland	194
Distant wars	195
Critique, Charles Clifford Brooks III	196
Worst wars	197
Critique, KC Bosch	198
Laze away the day	199
Critique, Ashok Karra	199
The law of attraction	204
Critique, Hans Ostrom	206

On walls	207
Critique, Bill Yarrow	208
Rich man, poor man	211
Critique, Carlene Tejada	212
Denial	213
Critique: Responsive writing, Maxwell Baumbach	213
Where is the justice in that?	215
Critique, John Gosslee	215
Well done	217
Critique, Walter Elmore	218
Original face	220
Critique, David B Axelrod	221
Injustice	224
Critique, Julie Ellinger Hunt	224
Critique: Responsive art, Julie Ellinger Hunt	225
Sand and photographs	229
Critique, Rae Spencer	230
Not there yet	234
Critique, Courtney Leigh Jameson	234
Second chances	240
Critique, Jena Salon	241
Failing	243
Critique, Kenneth Karrer	243
Critique: Responsive writing, Kenneth Karrer	245
Moving on	248
Carey High School bleachers	248
Critique: Responsive writing, Julie Ellinger Hunt	249
Critique: Responsive art, Julie Ellinger Hunt	250
Hell's kitchen	251
Critique, Andrew Badger	251
The strength of old ideals	254
Critique, Stan Galloway	254

Circles	256
Critique, David B Axelrod	257
Randomness near the end	259
Critique, Courtney Leigh Jameson	260
Here and hereafter	261
Critique, Gloria Mindock	261
Saltian	264
Critique, Laura C Lieberman	265
A-head	268
Critique, Annmarie Lockhart	268
Editorial Board Bios	273
About the Author	285

Saltian

Introduction

What an amazing miracle it is to be alive, to be actual, real, a creature of this planet, and more—a person connected to webs of other persons, to whole cosmologies of others: families, communities, societies, the entire history of humanity, written and unwritten. Alice Shapiro's histories, thankfully, are written. *Saltian "to dance"* is built upon the foundation of a famous soliloquy written by the unrivaled greatest writer of all time, William Shakespeare, but it's also built on experiences that are as universal among people as itches and the need to scratch them. *Saltian* is a baby's cry, a wedding song, a dirge, and everything in between.

The Roman emperor and philosopher Marcus Aurelius claimed that life is more like wrestling than dancing. A memorable line, no doubt, but if Aurelius had been given the opportunity to read Shapiro, he might have come to see the underlying dance in every wrestling match. Moreover, he might have realized that life is really more like dancing than wrestling.

In Olympic wrestling, opponents face each other in a circle, an island of sorts, and everything is very clear: the opponent is in plain sight, squaring off, and the rules are typically known and enforced. But in dancing, everyone is connected to everyone else in some way—they are all bound by the music or the beat and there are no islands and far fewer rules. Your own worst enemy on the dance floor may well be yourself or your best friend. Such is life. Shapiro both celebrates and mourns the dance of life unflinchingly and with aplomb, in no uncertain terms.

Alice Shapiro

Franz Kafka wrote, "a book must be the axe for the frozen sea within us." However, a book of poetry must be that and more. A book of poetry must do more than just hack out a fishing hole in us through which the talented angler may cast the fictive dream. A book of poetry must melt our frozen seas, turn them to vapor, and then let them fall back into ourselves as the earth and ore, diamond and coal of our inner lives. It must be transformative.

Saltian is a transformative book of poetry about the transformations that define human life. Beyond its structure of universal human experience, there is a rich tapestry of image and sound. Shapiro creates full worlds of experience through carefully crafted images as she makes music with her words. The result is a beautifully gardened labyrinth that leads through the soul into places that only each reader can discover—perhaps some readers will glimpse "the undiscovered country " Hamlet spoke of or perhaps they find themselves on a journey that was altogether unexpected, and as Kurt Vonnegut writes, "unexpected travel plans are dancing lessons from God."

Happy dancing.

Robert CJ Graves

Saltian

Preface

The poems in *Saltian* are loosely based on this monologue from Shakespeare's play, *As You Like It*.

All the world's a stage,
And all the men and women merely players;
They have their exits and their entrances;
And one man in his time plays many parts,
His acts being seven ages. At first the infant,
Mewling and puking in the nurse's arms;
And then the whining school-boy, with his satchel
And shining morning face, creeping like a snail
Unwillingly to school. And then the lover,
Sighing like a furnace, with a woeful ballad
Made to his mistress' eyebrow. Then a soldier,
Full of strange oaths, and bearded like the pard,
Jealous in honour, sudden and quick in a quarrel,
Seeking the bubble reputation
Even in the cannon's mouth. And then the justice,
In fair round belly with good capon lin'd,
With eyes severe and beard of formal cut,
Full of wise saws and modern instances;
And so he plays his part. The sixth age shifts
Into the lean and slipper'd pantaloon,
With spectacles on nose and pouch on side;
His youthful hose, well sav'd, a world too wide
For his shrunk shank; and his big manly voice,
Turning again toward childish treble, pipes
And whistles in his sound. Last scene of all,
That ends this strange eventful history,
Is second childishness and mere oblivion;
Sans teeth, sans eyes, sans taste, sans everything
—Jaques (Act II, Scene VII, lines 139-166)

Saltian

Seven mortal steps

Man, iron man formed of soil
teased, like a willow in the wind
by music and carnal intensity
who are you?

Myths of kingly deeds dissolve with time
moon-gods fade to cinematic phantoms
poised to thrill
and the sun goes down on ancient legends.

Some humans never question,
work hard to follow trends
unaware clothes go out of fashion
each season.

Anger, fear,
fierce and ardent feelings
swayed by moon's elusive passion
push the body towards destruction

and control this mortal dance:

1. Infancy

An infant's span
is spittle and a gurgling gut
jerked limbs fighting air
blank eyes, soft bones
sleep.

2. Childhood

A child grows tall
before mind reasons
and the awkward kiss of good and evil
becomes the adolescent's
clouded mirror.

3. Lover

In a lover's focus
all narrow and lust,
a beloved's conquest
is the single touch that matters.
Death's promise is feared not.

4. Soldier

Here is the land of the quarrel
where a soldier's stage
is of embattled villain and hero
and in the breast of combat
lies precision.

5. The Justice

Having come to wealth
displeasure dwarfs our joy
until it fizzles.
The couch is more familiar than the sky.
We sigh and grumble.

Saltian

6. The Pantaloon*, Old Age

Ancient now, we should be wise
from stress, strain, error.
Yet the plan remains a youthful scheme
wasting time, repeating hateful scenes
having love and loved ones leave.

7. Dementia and Death

Slow, hesitant we grope
to propel a weak ambition.
Acceptance overtakes our passions.
Watered eyes, soft bones
sleep

control this mortal dance.

It is a wonder then
that good and beneficial passage
from Age to Age
improves our lot.
Who and what, o mighty soul
has charmed you?

The Pantaloon is a character in the 16th century commedia dell'arte *portrayed as a foolish old man in tight trousers and slippers. In modern pantomime he is the foolish, vicious old man, the butt and accomplice of the clown.*

I. Infancy

An infant's span
is spittle and a gurgling gut
jerked limbs fighting air
blank eyes, soft bones
sleep.

> *A babe in the house is a well-spring of pleasure,*
> *a messenger of peace and love, a resting place for*
> *innocence on earth, a link between angels and men.*
> —Martin Farquhar Tupper
> English writer and poet (1810-1889)

Saltian

Entrance

And a child behaved as the angels.
It was a dream where he was lifted skyward
and floated higher than her brilliant body.

From there he saw that he was born
earth-bound, flesh, a man whose place,
attached to female, was meant to mark

her sacrifice
the gift of life.
This entering

accompanied by a verse simply sung
exploded with unearthly sound
and began with startled words:
I have a mother!

Alice Shapiro

Where are you?

> *My friend has a baby. I'm recording*
> *all the noises he makes so later I can ask*
> *him what he meant.*
> —Stephen Alexander Wright,
> American comedian

In curious times dreams were vivid.
I wondered where you were
between the misted twilight
before birth, before awareness.
Were you focused on your heartbeat
and bones that grow by increments
and hunger pangs and wetness
or does your mind stay mystical
holding on to vapors in a spirit realm
where love and soul are one?

I wondered, as in dreams,
was your flesh inert, your mind alert
traveling far beyond a solid field
yet recognizing furniture and trees
absent time, outside space
afloat in substanceless pursuit
like a twitching, napping dog
catching an imaginary adversary, cat.

Saltian

Is that you, child, flound'ring round the ether
waiting to be waked
to feel the touch of mother's breast
to see sun, moon, and seasons turn
hear brother's laughter
while split off from sense?
I think of God who sent a Son
through a narrow portal
linked to spirit, and fully manifest.
This is more than Heaven. It is your gift to descend.

Alice Shapiro

Look up at the green and blue

> *To sit in the shade on a fine day, and look up*
> *on verdure is the most perfect refreshment.*
>
> —Jane Austen
> from *Mansfield Park*

A carriage sways gently
from a summer wind
as two eyes, barely open
seize the sky
their baby blue caught
in the corner of a small awakening
heart.

Now, distracted by a rustling tree
an ear perceives rhythm
connects a leaf's green essence
with its sound
and tucks away this impression
so later it can be found
and named.

Who thinks the infant knows
what manifests is dear
and in some distant year
when faith is rather torn
and dawn hardly warms,
this idyllic spot
will be the rock?

Saltian

Grand Malia

Flower on this Earth
I first saw you shining
a royal glow charged
with beauty beyond
an ordinary birth
one small package wrapped
in precious jewels of essence.

I knew it then
I see it now.

It is certain that as you grow
with a gentle frown across your brow
kings will fall
to gather up your happiness
to lay their treasures in your
outstretched hand
to glance again upon your smile.

I knew it then
I see it now.

Babe, purely innocent
no ill deed or stain will tarnish you.
Dressed in God's raiment
you are blessed with love and loveliness
and if I could, I dare not influence
your choices.
A brilliant path is yours alone, and certain.

Alice Shapiro

INFANCY

In gratitude we welcome Grace
Near a grove of fragrant eucalyptus hidden
From a harsh world, underneath these trees of fortune
Awash with succulent, sweet fruit.
Now, before the multitude of wanderers and guests, we
Cannot cry out at sorrow.
Yeshua sent a child, we named her.

Saltian

End of the line

Mother, whose womb I leave
to breathe
whose voice was marred
by the irony of lung disease,
I wish I had studied you.

Mother, whose womb now bereft
of sentient life
I see with blackened lungs scarred by smoke.
Fears were cloaked in disregard
and you succumbed.

While in the throes of full dependence
needing only self-satisfaction
I missed your years of sacrifice.
Your never-ending warmth
was seen as being mine.

This offshoot then is dedicated
to all your decency and flaws, not followed
except for fitful lapses
that last until this child arrests
the lineage, stays barren.

Infant, infant

It is all soft when the hand
strokes an infant's skin.
When a palm glides along its tepid plane
a blast of innate love is felt.

One gets protective at the frailty of
complete dependence
exchanges depths of feeling
at first sight.

Can there be anything closer
than the stare a baby makes
in awe of discovering her mirror face?
A-gaggle at the wet tub water—
splashes, laughter, amazement!

Would that I in later years
could recall such infant scenes
instead of screams and hovering
in closets.

It is given to me
to un-remember
and to glory in the touch
of children.

II. Childhood

A child grows tall before mind reasons
and the awkward kiss of good and evil
becomes the adolescent's
clouded mirror.

> *There are children playing in the street who could solve*
> *some of my top problems in physics because they have*
> *modes of sensory perception that I lost long ago.*
> —J Robert Oppenheimer
> from *Pearls of Wisdom*

> *A lot of people insisted on a wall between modern dance*
> *and ballet. I'm beginning to think that walls are very*
> *unhealthy things.*
> —Twyla Tharp

Saltian

A cow woke me up

History floods a brain
suddenly upon
the hearing of old tunes.
That's how
this tale begins
dancing to
"The Farmer in the Dell."

One day I woke to find myself
in grammar school
in front of the room
but centered within the group's consciousness
attached, as to a womb
with many brothers, sisters
crowding, floating round.
One droning hum of learning
that bore no quality nor distinction, no fun.

Assigned a task to draw a cow
I copied fervently and well
and was rewarded loud and hearty
which took me from the spell
of sameness.
I was now "other"
different from the rest
better, I guessed
and a hefty ego stormed.

One step further to the wall
where I was told to draw
more cows and such
from memory.

Alice Shapiro

I stood then on my chair
to reach the heights
of physical and mental hierarchy.

I rose to the command, looking down
on rows of children stuck
in ordered mediocrity.
Prematurely celebrating my escape, I drew
but not a cow came through my crayoned hand.
I was drained of accuracy
alarmed at nullity
and the void where previously
I was kinged.

Jarred from sleep
into separation
into confused disappointment
I thought I was through
but shock became chagrin
as the very same admirer
who had such lengthy praise
one wide-eyed smile ago
now scolded in an angry tone.

It was too late for that
as this second birth
could not be taken back.
I would never be
an ordered row
of mediocrity again
for I had witnessed self.

Saltian

Why this, why that?

Why halt before the flame?
Why embrace the rain?

Discovery is strange, awesome
and a little ugly
like mud-pies and that first dirty
smoke.

The child opens up a closet door
the drawer flowered with appliqués
a white porcelain box that hides a locket.
She touches, looks, explores.

Questioning small things
that go ignored
by aged eyes and tired visions
she soaks in more, and more

becomes
the answer.

Alice Shapiro

Miss K's arabesque

> *I go a lot to see young people downtown*
> *in little theatres. It's great. If you start*
> *somebody's career, it's so exciting.*
> —Mikhail Baryshnikov

Pink leotards, net tutus
and little girls pirouette
raise up on satin pointe shoes at the barre
arch feet and backs
stretch arms as gracefully as instructed
so poise can be constructed
into their body's consciousness.

Then onto ballet slippers
soft black leatherette with rubber band straps
to *plié, chassé, jeté*
to twirl and leap and spin at season's end recital
where fairy dancers promenade, bob and weave
in not so regimented order as perceived
and choreographed by Miss K's virtuoso desire.

Back to class, to shiny, slick parquet
a childhood filled with ballerina,
tap, toe, acrobatic antics
and all the scenes, all these years remembered.
Yet I wonder why
not once did I envision life
on stage as a dancer.

Dysfunction

1.
Upon the resolution of a fight
between two adults in the clan
a child a-shiver in the corner
tries to understand
a frown or a sneer appearing
on the mouth that spews a happy
word, apologies, honor
after miscreants confuse the matter
saying one thing harboring another.

2.
It is almost fun to solve
a puzzle, unravel strings
of life's impeccable moments,
an Aha! a Wow! the how
you fit together. And when
you put a name to it, call it
gone, embellish or employ it
in dance or song, the dazzle
rights a wrong, sanctifies
a long-suppressed muddle.

Alice Shapiro

The sea intrudes and calms

A swim in frigid waters
whose threatening waves
dwarf a child of ten
caught by an undertow
where a sudden breathlessness
is thrust before him
and breath's function registers—
preparing him for death
and so many death scenes
that will creep into the years.
Thing is, he shows no fear
as limbs' tension disappears
in the float, in the enveloping
comfort that is the sea—
a liquid metaphor in which
the womb resurrects.
Eyes open to this intruding sea
he feels peace, thoughtlessness, one.

Saltian

The Feast of St. Catherine

In our vacant lot the carnival
burst into town each June
like a Verdi opera.

Pink gossamer to eat
mud-stomped grass beneath our feet
a shrill Italian song

emanating over children's jeers
the aim to win, to beat old carnys'
sleights against all odds.

      And the gambler's vice begins.

Day fades, lanterns light, a crowd wanders
circling tent-booths lined with wooden ducks
dead to barrels aimed to kill.

      And the gun for sport dawns.

We spin around on giant teacups
dizzy from the ride
take note of a faint, free mind

      And reach for sweet, indulgent wine.

At dusk, painted horses gallop on everlasting turns
help us grab the golden ring
and if our sense is strong enough

      A holy promise sings.

Alice Shapiro

Seeds

A summer bungalow awakes
as sunbeams peek through tattered curtains
and a three-year-old, crumpled under cotton covers
giggles at the friend her father introduces
as his sun-bronzed, muscled arms tickle her.
Desire forms and a sense of future
different than the entertaining toy
or a parent's unconditional comfort.

One day in a grown time
this same woman kneels to weed a garden.
A shadow blocks her light.
She turns, looks up
as two bright eyes peer down.
The neighbor's son at seven
silent and awakened
flowers.

III. Lover

In a lover's focus
all narrow and lust,
a beloved's conquest
is the single touch that matters.
Death's promise is feared not.

> *There is safety in reserve, but no attraction. One*
> *cannot love a reserved person.*
> —Jane Austin
> from *Emma*

Saltian

In the morning, looking

Cut from a family's cord
a first sweet lust-experiment
may last a mind's lifetime
despite a ruptured covenant.

Her adoration is swept up at the flush
of a warm cheek, her attention stolen
as she traces every line, studies with enchanted eyes
every muscle-bulge on a lover's thigh.

This isn't scrutiny.
It is an amorous regard
with not a drop of prejudice, nor preference.
It is a wonderment at the custody of love.

Alice Shapiro

Catching love

> *Happiness is a butterfly, which, when*
> *pursued, is always just beyond your*
> *grasp, but which if you will sit down*
> *quietly, may alight upon you.*
> —Nathaniel Hawthorne

Malaysian stew, too oily for enjoyment
is pushed aside.
She leaves the table
and the day-rain cannot stop her plan.

With great speed
she organizes artistic work in sections
labels, stacks, orders drawings
but the shelf stays sweeter than sweated-over, painted dreams.

Mid-life, mid-career
this frantic phase spans years
long away from him
and a peace once afforded two.

To think about the battle
to change from human love to hobby love
one wonders after having lost them both
which love is best to hunt?

Too young to sift through
a gold-weave basket of inherited traits
too old to labor for elusive truth
the ocean-tossed decade
stays a cache of passionate yearning.

Saltian

Where is the dance?

> *I think art education, especially*
> *in this country, which government*
> *pretty much ignores, is so important*
> *for young people.*
> —Mikhail Baryshnikov

Morning's drift puts him off
as dreams grasp at waking layers
the pull, pushing
sleep-eyes loath to wake—
there is money to make.

Endeav'ring to perform for Uncle Sam
he clownishly waltzes for recognition.
Stepped upon, shuffled over, crushed into the floor
he bears his sorrow and wilts like old cabbage leaves
unfit for sweet crunchy slaw.

> To put a foot out the door
> he drags his attitude forward
> claws his way to subsidized fortune
> ignoring former taps upon
> a wished-for dance career.

Years pass.
He forgets his passion while wrapped
in cuddled layers of temporary coupling.
Side-tracked, strength waning
he missteps toward tradition.

Alice Shapiro

The transparency of a Spanish fly

In Acapulco
ten years after
a loosed marriage-bed
she sat alone at the edge
of a flower-patterned sofa
reverie interrupted
when a younger pair took
the other cushion
unaware of her presence.

> Cooing like a cockatiel in heat
> the sexy lady rambled on
> with a Castilian beat
> talking up what seemed
> ordinary speech

Being peripheral and nonexistent
she observed with blatant courage
their love-dance.

> He begged, he pleaded
> his question unheeded
> and her bleating chatter
> bleeding on his persistence.

Neither woman budged.
The hot sun went down.
At the same moment they both knew
his infant frown and escalating ardor
must be caught
like a fly in a sticky viscid trap.

Saltian

She picked the ripe fruit
and with an imperceptible smile
it was over.
They left the couch
hand in hand.
An elevator took them up
doors closed on hasty exploration.

Alone again, she wished that she
had sipped this liquor sooner.

Jealous plate

Under an umbrella'd bistro
wild geese passing by
I peered skyward, backward.
Why?

A plea from once-kissed lips ...

Where is the absent occupant
whose chair should be energized
with laughs and conversation
exchanging giddy romances?

The prize escaped, dined elsewhere.

One dinner came
luxurious, on heated china.
I ate politely
thinking hate.

I saw her arms entangled round his wrist.

Pretzel-twisted feelings rose
accompanied by my swallow-gulps
of undigested Bourbon shrimp.
I drowned in angered waters

cursed Fate.

The salve of women meeting

I came
anticipated
ate and drank.

We entered into lively chats
laughed and cried
bonded.

Women in the field
in the depth of ascension

business, business done
profit by embracing wisdom
in a similar realm.

Support, comfort
shared adventures
and we glide through silt

sludge, sediment,
and help quash tattered worn-out theories
exhale, stroke the sun.

Alice Shapiro

Desire

> *A friend is a second self*
>
> —Aristotle

> *The cries of Lois*
> *the dearth of shame*
> *the help of brothers*
> *the force of disdain*
> *the books of poets*
> *the poems of rain*
>
> —Alice Shapiro, post meridiem

I cannot tell whether
diamonds appeared in his eyes
or mine
as the shine of adoration
became the icon
one sees in history
a Byzantine sparkle
Medieval armor against all odds.

We stand on stages
act our play
sometimes alone in our heads
      (before the mating)
sometimes in platitudes and lies
      (after years together).
I recognize the dew
and the frost.

Saltian

Can you come to me innocent
each day, each moment
where a diamond's glint
appears as highlights
between your words
between our silences
as we lie down
in fields of smiles?

IV. Soldier

Here is the land of the quarrel
where a soldier's stage
is of embattled villain and hero
and in the breast of combat
lies precision.

> *What would it mean if there were a theory that explained everything? And just what does "everything" actually mean, anyway? Would this new theory in physics explain, say the meaning of human poetry? Or how economics work? Or the stages of psychosexual development? Can this new physics explain the currents of ecosystems, or the dynamics of history, or why human wars are so terribly common?*
> —Ken Wilbur
> from *A Theory of Everything:*
> *An Integral Vision for Business,*
> *Politics, Science and Spirituality*

A son's war

Soldier, soldier
babe with gun
with angel cheeks
of rosy hue
barely loosed
from love's embrace
engaged in war
protects a country.

Sweat gathering
from the hike
in heat
in mud
and hill upon hill.
Time slows down
day turns dark
prayers before the fight.

Finally the strike.
The mark—a shocked foe
stares back
at the bullet's source
caressing wishes
of surrender
to prison
instead of Death.

Alice Shapiro

Not my war

My first soldier was my father.
The second I married.
In between I'd see a few
        here and there in supermarkets
        and on the television
        but mostly passing by
as I offered hasty thank-yous
and after two broad, proud smiles
I to my kitchen
he to the fire.

Daddy died from alcohol.
Joe's brain got cancer.
I'll never know his outcome
or if my words mattered.

Corporate war zones

One desk quiet
with an open book
cradled in between
two fatted, idle hands
aside another desk
pressured to fulfill
dull tasks
at high speeds,
perfectly executed, is

un-
even
justice.

Four white walls
lacking ventilation
choke down indignation
act as crowds whose voice
can snuff the swimmer
drown the floater.
They speak the motto:
Standard blueprints rule.
Don't digress.

Absorb that.
Do not praise the salmon
besieged in homebound waters.

Alice Shapiro

Fame prevails
despite the droning
efforts to suppress
for the worthy ones
like VP Wallace Stevens,
Albert Einstein patent king,
some unnamed, yet-
to-be-discovered
scholar.

Still, one wonders
do inner battles
birth better art?

Saltian

Street wars

She stole the name
of one thought dead
not wanting her own work
enlisted in the Army
saved her comrade's life

declined a hero's medal
so as not to state
illegal deeds
with a searching, lurking
INS.

A young man saw her
in the neighborhood.
He idolized and followed
then felt uneasy
but stuffed his scruples down.

Torn away from law
exemplified by her acts
he reached for wrong behavior
bought fake ids
drugged and drank
was brought to justice
sentenced for infractions.

Alice Shapiro

Confusion and unanswered questions
slid down his gut.
A sudden terror rose
until a displaced anger chose the gun
that fired at a harmless crowd.
Unaware, uncaring
she had set him up.

Armed with righteous indignation
we spat at them,
but who decided it was best
to see or do nothing
before the taking of their criminal acts?

Saltian

After war

Not a fan of war
I abhor violence in all its peculiarities
yet the warrior who fights injustice
knows about evil.

A bully must be beat
in a language understood
or thwarted like Mahatma did.
Where are the saints, the solvers?

In the ranks,
trenches, holes
battling one on one
the horror

then coming home to concrete sorrow
wondering for the children destined
to cause the morbid death
of flesh again.

Poised in a corner, covering his knees
blazing eyes turn terrified.
The enemy within his head
nests and festers.

Beneath a crumbling wall
cold, a hand extended for a dime
he sings, surrenders to the rain
remembering the heat of battle.

It is a shame.

Alice Shapiro

Distant wars

> *You cannot simultaneously prevent*
> *and prepare for war*
> —Albert Einstein

Behind a soldier's half-dimmed eyes
jungle shrieks fly, bat-like
swooping at his back.
Surprised, his heart cries
races
alert.
Home, he is safe.
Rivals reconcile, forget—
but not him at night
when carrion in dreams appear.
In time, mind's curtain blocks
the dwindling shadows
and love learns to walk.

Sons and daughters trade their freedom
for us.

Encrypted screens
in digital form
blast off legs, arms.
We are safe.
No harm comes at a green distance
from giving killing signals.
The game remains
a general's numbing verbal order.

Sons and daughters learn a trade.

Saltian

Worst wars

A cancerous child desired to be a soldier.
Granted this, he spent a day and night
in bivouacs, rifle drills, exercising
in and out of rubber tires
scaling walls with a gentle lift
from combat buddies.
His lit-up face among the giants
towering over his frailty
was prize enough for those who organized
his brief and poignant tour of duty.

Most young boys imagining a toy war
go home to dinner
with all four limbs, bullet-free abdomens
and scar-less psyches
unlike a soldier's life
that is envied unaware of consequences.

And so a country's choices must
bear delicate scrutiny
while sending idealistic soldier-boys and girls
to foreign lands
to disarm the enemy, to protect us,
and God forbid, to die.

The child whose illness
brought him early access
to a war zone
in the fore-days of his death
died happy, free
of more than one reality.

V. The Justice

Having come to wealth
displeasure dwarfs our joy
until it fizzles.
The couch is more familiar than the sky.
We sigh and grumble.

> *You're going to go completely drunk because*
> *you're nuts with power.*
> —Dr C Hewitt
> Educator, Theoretical Physics

> *I say more: the just man justices;*
> *Keeps grace: that keeps all his goings graces;*
> *Acts in God's eye what in God's eye he is—*
> *Christ—for Christ plays in ten thousand places,*
> *Lovely in limbs, and lovely in eyes not his*
> *To the Father through the features of men's faces.*
> —Gerard Manley Hopkins

Saltian

Laze away the day

Love morning
late and lazy
love that

cat curling
up bottom of the bed
not time yet

sun washes
over sheets and pillows
approaching noon

June summers
perplex the dead-
hearted nay-sayers

who jump at dawn
to be machines
collapse at dusk

bedding none
of their dreams
they run to work again.

Alice Shapiro

The law of attraction

> *A man is like a cat, chase him and*
> *he will run—sit still and ignore him*
> *and he'll come purring at your feet.*
> —Helen Rowland

This is the abstract:
Within reach
the prize hovers
yet still she hides a former lack
as someone else's fare.

Almost there,
she wonders where the change began
between the stress of get it, get it
and the seamless streaming flow.

She was knighted without her knowledge
without attention or control.
It is hard to let go
easy to slip, like a drunkard denying drink

back to active force through effort.
She knows that batter must be stirred
by human hands
but only fire bakes sweet cakes.

This is the tale:
A man of former wealth, now vagabond
who suffered sudden lapses into dark mind
once taught a girl a lesson
more kind than cash.

Saltian

He commanded her to stillness
while first he cursed
the wife who sealed
his present prison fate.

Continuing, he berated mother
for committing him to Hell
upon his former spouse's
unjust recommendation.

The curious crowd noticed from nearby
as if they were swayed by a Syrian flute
that wakes a sleeping snake
and glued their eyes to his dramatic, irate state.

He rambled. She listened.

The rock of sheer solid steady sitting
caused awe and interest
did not betray the fact that here
there was mostly nothing.

She saw how attitude begets impressions
and slowed-down actions
bring attention away from there
towards here.

This is the outcome:
Equal in mental disfiguration
they gained a bond.
Years passed.

Alice Shapiro

An intruding link from that distance
recalled the wisdom she now needed
that a sad and fractured millionaire once imparted.

He mentored her
and proved that when in need
she should emulate the loss of tension

which activates the future
blessed, unharmed, lucrative,
charmed.

On walls

Onto the far wall
as I lounge in bed
I create imaginary
fanciful stripes and spotty squares.
My head satisfies a compulsion
to order everything
to place objects
in spaces whose cool effects
may please the eye.

Dressing for the day, I remember
walls so covered do not breathe.
"Leave them bare," I scold myself
so when the impulse
coaxes like a drug
I should resist, instead
I see the imperfection
of dried white paint
blistering off the wall.

The Abstract Expressionists
must have seen these flaws
as they swept away
their rigid, ordering past
leaving scratches, Pollock drips
exploding shapes and colors
from DeKooning's brush
Non-conforming visions—
the life of paint on walls.

Alice Shapiro

Rich man, poor man

Wise-cracking razzers saw fine proverbs
wise-ass crows are loud as a neighbor's chanticleer
they all speak sly like Pharisees before the cleansing.

The satiated merchant
rests upon his brocade chair
goaded on by hangers-on.
Having gathered wealth and fame
he crosses arms above his bloated gut
not knowing if his friend is present
for short advice, high chatter duty
or for a share of this man's money cache.

As if from a deep black hole
alone, he looks back wondering:
Given this poor end
would a different path
have offered satisfaction,
a wife and children
instead of boundless circles
of sycophants?

Too late. It is done, this career.
He awaits another stage to appear
to teach elusive, unachievable perfection.

Saltian

Denial

When one has done most everything
that a childish mind desires—

white-haired and haberdashered
the thread about to unravel
the chink in the champagne glass
about to lengthen
subordinates' sneers increasing,
attrition in its infancy
is quietly noticed

and pushed down like so much salt
stuck at ocean's bottom.

Alice Shapiro

Where is the justice in that?

Young minds think mature
despite a jumbled slew of words spat out.
Amazed at the wisdom of babes
one wonders is it fair
that word cells die when aged
leaving spaces where once lay places
of good times spent
names and faces rent of links
to anything?

Attacked, that child felt insult
formed a brash response
strong enough to drain the blood
but lacked a physical skill to mouth it.
Common now in her old age
we hear the loud and gritty verbal grumbles
near every neighbor's exit
replace her former lack of reprimand
as if berating all for childhood errors.

Where is the justice in that?

Well done

I.   Presently

I—peruse past decades
I—have accomplished greatness
I—overcame
- arcane banality
- self-doubt
- impetuous naivete

Tender errors at ten and twenty
baked onto inner walls of an open mind
formed a calloused heart.

II.   Looking back

Barefoot
walking sand-drenched sidewalks in the tropics
dazed, yet unfazed by a temporary lapse
in continuity

God—at my back

- arcane banality—self-doubt
- went up like smoke.

III.   Future

Purified
wise wide innocence shares my easy chair
I—consider grace.

VI. The Pantaloon, Old-Age

Ancient now, we should be wise
from stress, strain, error.
Yet the plan remains a youthful scheme
wasting time, repeating hateful scenes
having love and loved ones leave.

> *For what do we live, but to make sport for our neighbors,*
> *and laugh at them in our turn?*
>
> —Jane Austen
> from *Pride and Prejudice*

Saltian

Original face

> *If I had only known,*
> *I would have been a locksmith.*
>
> —Albert Einstein

The pale, exotic man
white flakes scattered on his shoulders
walks the foyer, sweeps over
marble squares in flip-toed satin slippers.

Mutton-stuffed, olive-pitted, four-course full
and flabby, he drops heavy on a velvet cushion.
A sigh of woes blows, like opium smoke
through the iron filigree partition. He reclines
sees his dark-ringed orbs reflected in a mirror.

Glassy eyes look past the fault and flicker
at each grumble.

—the note that's due
—the errant worker
—the crumbling empire

How long it stood, a fine Fort Knox
building gold, prospering empty pockets.

The fire's dying, crimson embers fade
and a gray chill begets a hemorrhage of reckoning.
He sees, in one gloss
the dream before the dream.

Injustice

I might assume you mean to say
I am lovely and dear
and once I would have been assured
of this.

Now you stare, blank and faraway
more salient thoughts beckon your attention.

I could ramble endlessly
about fantastic things
and you would simply nod
agreeably.

Open those eyes and look, look again!
I am here and waiting for your refrain.

Sing it, speak it low and indistinct
but gather muster just this once
allow my dried, outdated illusions
like a fashion faux pas not yet new and chic.

I pause.
You leave.

Saltian

Photographs and sand

His grown son's photo
taken at a lovely beach
we both knew
rested now in my view.

His name drawn in sand
caused a feeling
and it was seized
fast without considering
without propriety.
I looked and looked
trembling.

I scrutinized the photo
awaited recognition
but what peered back
was silence.
This was not my child
nor my soul.
He was hers.

It did not matter.
Beach sand scratched on frozen film
can't be washed away by an ocean.
One can look as often as one wants
to see that name
recapture loving
a taste of salt hinting
at what could have been.

Alice Shapiro

It did not matter.
Almost gone, like his smile
upon my entrance
the scratches in beach sand
spelling out his name
are frozen eternally on film.
The ocean will never wash away
every microscopic trace of him
and one can look as often as one wants
to see that name, recapture loving
a taste of salt hinting at what could have been.

Saltian

Not there yet

I hear of some who live eight decades
hear their bones creak like dried, splintered stairs
see morning's strained and pained movements
while they step gingerly into a porcelain tub
not royally bathed in milk like Cleopatra.

They wail at forgotten faces they cannot place
as if erased and unborn.
Who can come to them at ninety
replace a broken body, restore dead cells
that once replenished, built strength?

Their fresh and active children
uninitiated yet to such a future Fate
deride the old, unattractive gait
laying down beneath their feet
the ones who raised them up.

Far off, I hear a strained lament:
Old age ain't no picnic.
I barely hear my inner clock
while in the thick of project after project
and contemplate instead my full and fancy state.

Alice Shapiro

Second chances

Younger girl
In this particular case
much time passed
in solitary confinement
not chained inside a physical prison
parted from the world by bars and guards
but hidden in the corner of an eye
whose depth and breadth of vision
delved far in only one direction—within
like a searchlight on a lonely
lighthouse sandbar
spying distant shipwrecks
searching for a sign of life.

Apparently no act could change a thing
except to pick up floating broken pieces.

An old girl
Like a child develops
to one day see
words appear from single letters,
this old crone was shocked to find
a body connected to her head
not within a physical structure
of sinew and bone
but vibrant in the world of flowers,
hours spent with friends
doing what were once
merely wishful thoughts colliding, parting
like atoms in a cell.

Saltian

Now the promise has come true
these separate parts, a whole.

Down to earth
The glue of mind
expanding
ruling
who we are
sealing
what phase of
darkness
it is our time
to overcome
arrives
incrementally
on its own.

Alice Shapiro

Failing

Sweated palms holding on a ballroom banister
jerk along, a wobbling testament to
an old building high-held, once laughter-filled
with great music rising towards a tin-embossed ceiling.

It is a good match to knees that meet each step
with trepidation, anticipating a stumbling destiny
distant from the child whose fearless legs flew
on a first staircase, top to bottom.

It is partly memory
hardly stored in the cells of bones
now bowed and softened
no cushion for a fall.

I long for the spirit body of health
of strength, no pain, no disintegration
and aim to live this day as if
I am in heaven.

Moving on

Bring on the aphorisms
the diet pills
drape the mirror darkly, in chiffon
to hide a glimpse of aging skin
lusterless, droopy eyes
double chin.

In youth the flesh is weak
near death it is loose
on shrinking bones
a gradual warning
meant to ease transition
from faulty flesh to spirit zones.

Oldness is cold to the clinging eye
but warm, knowing that upon selection
one is soon to meet
the Holy Presence
and soon to be
breathing young again.

VII. Dementia and Death

Slow, hesitant we grope
to propel a weak ambition.
Acceptance overtakes our passions.
Watered eyes, soft bones
sleep

control this mortal dance.

Who ordered that?

—Isidor I Rabi
on the discovery of the muon

Saltian

Carey High School bleachers

Having descended an inch
from a previous height
to view the football field
eyes must peer atop
a horde of spectators' spectacles
to have the widest view ...
From bleachers, a grandchild's grandeur
gets blurred and embittered
by the nonsense of age.

From this oligarchic perch
the old woman
distracted from quarterback, cheerleaders,
pomp and circumstance
follows the hawk up, up.
While a crowd's roar fades away
she sniffs the joy of new grass
goes back into the cocoon of
faraway youth

coddles her
coddles everyone's
ageless spirit.

Alice Shapiro

Hell's kitchen

His accent reeks New York
that high-energy island
where a daily frenzied pace can kill
soot collects on window sills
sharing nostrils with cocaine.

Abuse eventually knocks you down
even faded body paint
branded into forearms
extracts metallic pain
when pulsing through an MRI machine.

He takes to bed to rest and cower
most unlike his youthful zeal
when sheets and pillows wildly scattered
o'er a city's floor
as he explored a lover's bower.

Saltian

The strength of old ideals

The pain, the pain
the pain, the pain
the pain
of eighty-eight

is calmed
only by such meditations I can muster
as the tale of fishermen I see
from my summer balcony.

The ramblings of my day's events
prevents her body's
dwelling on
monstrous unpleasantness.

I wonder when her tolerance will fade
and a crackling exhortation to the Lord
burst out her drawn shut mouth?
I have seen lesser men succumb.

Alice Shapiro

Circles

My neighbor is ninety-two
and sad to say
discredits every knock
and friendship
at the door.

She is sure, as if
her once kaleidoscopic eyes
that scrutinized pretty mirrors
still prove that hate
won't harm.

Her backwards view
remains untouched
by Death's immanence
as she stays unchanged
demanding just perfection.

I forbid myself this future, or
so intend, but if I reach her
long-lived end
please forgive an aged
parent's petty flaw.

Saltian

Randomness near the end

a.
I wonder, between one chaos
and another will I lose a grip
have insane screaming fits
forget when it is time to bring
the trash to curb on Sunday eve?

b.
A late sun empties its dwindling warmth
onto my shoulder
so I may drench my soul with heat
confirm a belief that life ends well
align my gratitude with the inner smile
of one who knows the undeserved sometimes reap
what others sow
        a life of toil, wrong attitudes,
        unproductive moves, unrelenting descents
        into oblivion must be sent packing

c.
From a perch on a bent tree
dangling on a fragile branch
wondering if a leap will bring a fall
or flight into another wondrous conquest,
eyes close, ablaze.

Alice Shapiro

Here and hereafter

At times past sixty
glimpses of the human's exit
strike a sudden chord
start me wondering
and I go somewhere
inexplicable
for just an instant.

I expect to pile these keepsakes
one upon another
until acceptance
crafts a picture
like a mason builds a house
we decorate and clutter
then throw doors wide in invitation.

Eventually we leave
the incompleteness
and loose it all, to rest
                      to fly within.

Saltian

**Saltian
(old English word meaning "to dance")**

*

Eyes of sixty-five remember lessons
clearer than a school child.
Old clumps of pain-visions accumulate
outdated, worn like 45 vinyl songs
along with joyful thoughts
peaks and valleys, strong
photo'd footholds from the past.

*

The shock of body parts decaying
daily aches and rising pains
begin the seventh deconstruction.
Mid-decade is assuaged by
resignation and reprieves
the truth of age is neatly disregarded
the future quietly ignored.

*

The ear of eighty
folds in on itself
as present sounds and conversations lapse.
A hidden chamber filled with wet dreams
rises to the top. Lost senses brew again
from that squirreled-away
often nasty trap.

Alice Shapiro

*

Not ripe enough to leap and twirl
our mind still dances
as milk-white bones of ninety—
porous, brittle, bent
these rounded immanent fossils—
dip towards the earth until they shed the law
and their temporary birth.

*

Freed from dirt-encumbered bodies
light-forms at their youthful peak
travel easy, eat the fruit
of health, well-being, truth
and are an everlasting dance
uncontaminated, evil being blotted out
like acrid smoke rising from the spit.

Postscript

> *What I am going to tell you about is what we teach our physics students in the third or fourth year of graduate school ... It is my task to convince you not to turn away because you don't understand it ... That is because I don't understand it. Nobody does.*
> —Richard P Feynman
> QED, The Strange Theory of Light and Matter
> Nobel Lecture, 1966

Alice Shapiro

A-head

Beating footprints on concrete
leaves marks and shadows if we turn to look.
The neck, curious as Lot's wife
commands reversal
and possible blockage to a pleasant walk.
The head, that fragile instrument of peace and evil
guides and reasons, soothes, abuses
invests, invites, deletes.
Mine in particular is king
or queen subordinating limbs
and organs, feet
do its bidding.

I am my head.
It is sometimes red and wrathful
green and cool
it takes me where it wants to
an everlasting tool
like driver's education school.
I cannot turn it off
even if it acts The Fool.
I plan to take it with me
in its spirit body
when a head no longer rules
this solitary earthly journey.

Appendix. Original Poems With Critiques

Note:

The original poems appear here, in order of their appearance in the original manuscript (still retained in this book). Following each poem is the critique, responsive work, and reader comments as they were originally posted at unbound CONTENT's bookblog (booksblog.unboundcontent.com).

The posts at the bookblog remain open to commentary and we continue to welcome feedback from readers at any point during their time with *Saltian*.

Saltian

Seven mortal steps

Man, iron man formed of soil,
teased, like a willow in the wind
by music and carnal intensity
who are you?

Myths of kingly deeds dissolve with time
moon-gods fade to cinematic phantoms
poised to thrill
and the sun goes down on ancient legends.

Some humans never question
work hard to follow trends
unaware clothes go out of fashion
each season.

Anger, fear,
fierce and ardent feelings
swayed by moon's elusive passion
push the body toward destruction.

and control this mortal dance:

    1. Infancy

An infant's span
is spittle and a gurgling gut
jerked limbs fighting air
blank eyes, soft bones
sleep.

2. Childhood

A child grows tall
before mind reasons
and the awkward kiss of good and evil
becomes the adolescent's
clouded mirror.

3. Lover

In a lover's focus
all narrow and lust,
a beloved's conquest
is the single touch that matters.
Death's promise is feared not.

4. Soldier

Here is the land of the quarrel
where a soldier's stage
is of embattled hero and villain
and in the breast of combat
lies precision.

5. The Justice

Having come to wealth
displeasure dwarfs our joy
until it fizzles.
The couch is more familiar than the sky.
We sigh and grumble.

Saltian

6. The Pantaloon, Old Age*

Ancient now, we should be wise
from stress, strain, error.
Yet the plan remains a youthful scheme
wasting time, repeating hateful scenes
having love and loved ones leave.

7. Dementia and Death

Slow, hesitant we grope
to propel a weak ambition.
Acceptance overtakes our passions.
Watered eyes, soft bones
sleep

control this mortal dance.

It is a wonder then
that good and beneficial passage
from Age to Age
improves our lot.
Who and what, o mighty soul
has charmed you?

*The Pantaloon—a character in the 16th century *commedia dell'arte*, portrayed as a foolish old man in tight trousers and slippers. In modern pantomime, the foolish, vicious old man, the butt and accomplice of the clown.

Alice Shapiro

Critique: Responsive writing
It Is not Sweet nor Proper: A Vision of Seven Mortal Steps
By Robert CJ Graves

Today a baby is born in the Coil.
Whose baby? Yours, but not yours,
just like every other baby.

And we see the child now, a 1950s boy
leaving the Saturday matinee cowboy serial.
He carries a toy gun, and Christmas will never come.

But soon the smell of autumn brings him to high school
and the scent of that certain girl's hair sends him
to a warm star and fills him with desire to be a man.

And then his childhood was just a sweet dream.
He awakens a soldier; he carries a machine gun
through jungles to that lonely place/time on the hill.

Back home, parents sigh and fizzle,
their joy killed on some foreign hill, "pro patria."
"It is not sweet, nor proper," they mutter.

So another of yours-but-not-yours is gone, and we are old.
We should have been wise for growing so old,
but the angry ways continue.

Dementia and demented acceptance stomps from DC
and Tehran and Beijing and Moscow and London and on
into the next Waterloo, the next Little Bighorn, the next Hiroshima.

Saltian

First entrance

And a child behaved as the angels.
It was a dream where he was lifted skyward
and floated higher than her brilliant body.

From there he saw that he was born
earth-bound, flesh, a man whose place,
attached to female, was meant to mark

her sacrifice
the gift of life.
This entering

accompanied by a verse simply sung
exploded with unearthly sound
and began with startled words:
"I have a mother."

Critique
By Ray Brown

I absolutely love this poem—am intrigued by it. At first I was put off by the title—seemed to foreshadow for some reason, a sexual encounter. After reading the poem, it now can have duel meaning—can be read one of two ways. Perhaps entrance into the world—entrance into life. I am not sure what the author intended. If it were my decision, I would drop the word "First" and simply call the poem "Entrance."

The beauty of this poem is the dynamic of its words. They live well together, coalesce in my mind, capture my heart and intrigue my intellect. They make me want to read more of the writer's work.

Alice Shapiro

Where are you?

> *My friend has a baby. I'm recording*
> *all the noises he makes so later I can ask*
> *him what he meant.*
> —Stephen Alexander Wright,
> American comedian

Where are you
in twilight just between
birth and awareness of earthbound objects?
Are you focused on your heartbeat
and bones that grow by increments
and hunger pangs and wetness
or does your mind stay mystical
holding on to vapors in a spirit realm
where love and soul are one?

In curious times dreams were vivid.
I wondered where one goes at sleep
the flesh inert, the mind alert
traveling far beyond a solid field
yet recognizing furniture and trees
absent time, outside space
afloat in substanceless pursuit
like a napping dog twitches
to catch an imaginary enemy, cat.

Is that you, child, flound'ring round the ether
waiting to be waked
to feel the touch of mother's breast
to see sun, moon, seasons turn
hear brother's laughter
while split off from sense?
This is more than Heaven. It is our gift to descend.
Was Christ's sacrifice to become as us
like your transitioned, dancing form—

linked to spirit, not fully manifest?

Critique
By Lynne Thompson

It's a daunting task to be asked to comment on a single poem without the entire manuscript available to determine how the poems work together. Nevertheless, I press on.

As I read and re-read "Where are you," I kept returning to the line "In curious times, dreams were vivid." It struck me that the line would be a knockout entry into the poem and arguably a more mysterious (read: intriguing) way into the poem without giving away too much of its meat, particularly in light of the epigraph Alice selected.

Of course, once I moved that compelling line to the beginning of the poem, I started playing around with all of the stanzas and the order in which they appear. The question, to my mind, is

Alice Shapiro

what line is going to pull me through to the next line and then, on to the next poem. The task put me in mind of Stephen Dobyn's collections of essays, *Best Words, Best Order*, and, in particular, his statement "[n]ot only do we read by anticipating what's coming next, we read through the lens of what we have read." Of course, the thrill of that anticipation is best fulfilled when we are met with a surprise. It was this tactic that lead me to rearrange the lines in "Where are you" and to make small tweaks in syntax and to delete lines that seemed less surprising, seemed more telling, not showing:

Where are you?

> *My friend has a baby. I'm recording*
> *all the noises he makes so later I can ask*
> *him what he meant.*
> —Stephen Alexander Wright,
> American comedian

In curious times dreams were vivid.
Where are you in twilight just between
birth and awareness
of the flesh inert, the mind alert
traveling far beyond a solid field—
recognizing furniture and trees
absent time, outside space
afloat in substanceless pursuit
like a napping dog twitching
to catch his imaginary enemy, cat.

Saltian

Is that you, child, flound'ring round the ether
waiting to be waked
to see sun, moon, and seasons turn,
hear brother's laughter
while split off from sense?
Are you focused on your heartbeat
and bones that grow by increments
and hunger pangs and wetness
or does your mind stay mystical
holding onto vapors in a spirit realm
where love and soul are one?

This is more than Heaven. It is our gift to descend.

Reader comments

Sarah wrote:
Wow! I love the way the beautiful lines of this poem are showcased by Lynne's reshuffling and tweaking, powerfully building up to the question, " ... does your mind stay mystical/holding onto vapors in a spirit realm/where love and soul are one?"

Alice Shapiro

Look up at the green and blue

> *To sit in the shade on a fine day, and look up*
> *on verdure is the most perfect refreshment.*
> —-Jane Austen

A carriage sways gently from a summer wind
as two eyes, barely open
seize the sky
its baby blue caught
in the corner of a small awakening
heart.

Now, distracted by a rustling tree
an ear perceives rhythm
connects a leaf's green essence
with its sound
and tucks away this impression
so later it can be found
and named.

Who thinks the infant knows
what manifests is dear
and in some distant year
when faith is rather torn
and dawn hardly warms,
this idyllic spot
will be
the rock?

Critique
By Bobbie Troy

I love the concept of the "dance of life" for this collection and look forward to reading the book. After all, we as poets, should strive to do just what Alice has done: capture what we have experienced or imagined about all of life's stages.

In this visual, multilayered poem, Alice introduces the Infancy stage of life, the ordinary that really is the extraordinary. She portrays the awakening of the heart and how the brain perceives the world and stores impressions. The language is superb. The reader can feel the gentle sway of the carriage and hear the rustling tree. Then the last stanza foreshadows what will come later in life as nature and infancy mature: "this idyllic spot will be the rock" that hopefully will restore lost faith and warm the dawn once again. I continued to get more from this poem each time that I read it. I would not change one word. The only suggestion I have is to add that the Jane Austen quotation is from *Mansfield Park*.

Alice Shapiro

Malia

Flower on this Earth
I first saw you shining
a royal glow charged
with beauty beyond
an ordinary birth
one small package wrapped
in precious jewels of essence.

I knew it then
I see it now.

It is certain that as you grow
with a gentle frown between your brow
kings will fall
to gather up your happiness
to lay their treasures in your
outstretched hand
to glance again upon your smile.

I knew it then
I see it now.

Babe, purely innocent
no stain or ill deed will tarnish you.
Dressed in God's raiment
you are blessed with love and loveliness
and if I could, I dare not influence
your choices.
A brilliant path is yours alone, and certain.

Critique
By Carlene Tejada

Alice Shapiro's tender poem about the arrival of a new life describes our hopes and dreams as we observe the perfection of newborns and the very young.

Three 7-line stanzas are separated by the repetition of a drumbeat-like couplet (4 strong 1-syllable words to a line). These 2 lines act like an announcement or oration. They are at home here with the fantasies of royal glow, jewels, kings, treasures. Alliteration and internal rhyme throughout the poem give a soft lyrical quality. For example, initial "b" and "p" in the first stanza, "ow" in the second stanza and "n" and "s" sounds in the third. Additional resonance occurs in the first stanza with "Earth," "first," and "birth"; and in the second stanza with "hand" and "glance." Such internal resonance and rhyme add rich layers to a poem. Alice does this very well.

One suggestion is to rethink use of the word "between" in the second stanza. "Between" means in a frame of two, and "brow" is singular. I confess to reading the poem three times to realize Malia is a baby, not a flower or place. All in all, this is a gentle and loving poem, a pleasure to read.

I.N.F.A.N.C.Y.

In gratitude we welcomed Grace
Near a grove of eucalyptus hidden
From a harsh world
Awash with fragrant trees and sweet fruit.
Now we do not
Cry out at sorrow.
Yeshua sent a child, we named her.

Critique
By Andrew Badger

Criticism: analyzing, classifying, interpreting, or evaluating literary or other artistic works.

I'll begin with some comments/suggestions. First, I see no justification for the periods in the title. In fact, they seem a distraction. Second, the phrase "Awash with fragrant trees" modifies world in the phrase "hidden from a harsh world." So I'd revise ll. 2-4 to read

> Near a grove of eucalyptus awash in
> Fragrant trees with sweet fruit
> And hidden from a harsh world.

Third, I feel that I'm looking at a shard of tile that will be worked into a mosaic, but I cannot see either the whole picture or even any of the adjacent tiles. Thus my evaluation and analysis may be spurious, specious, or suppositious.

Saltian

At first this short, seven-line, 37-word acrostic poem seems naive, perhaps even simplistic. But the more I read the poem—with or without my suggested emendations—the more three words clamored for attention: *Grace, eucalyptus,* and *Yeshua.* The more I dwelt on the meanings of those words, the more layers of meaning I saw in the simple words and phrases. I will begin with eucalyptus. Some of the mythological associations of eucalyptus are good fortune from the oil or wearing the wood and an aid in divinations. The gender association is feminine, clean and pure like mother earth from which eucalyptus is born.

Now I will deal with Grace, then tie Grace and Yeshua together. I am assuming that Grace is the name of the child Yeshua sent. In Christian theology Grace means *unearned or unmerited favor from God.* Our redemption is not quid pro quo (I do good and receive my wages in salvation); it is freely and deliberately given by Jesus (Rom 3:4, 5:15, et al). And Yeshua is the name Mary, Joseph, Peter, Paul, etc. called Jesus. Our society gives names to children to honor ancestors or to satisfy our sense of euphony. But in Hebrew culture, names had meanings which helped define the person named. And Yeshua means salvation. So, in the poem, our Jesus sends Grace to the feminine eucalyptus grove where life is awash with fragrance and sweet fruits.

Reader comments

Stan wrote:
Andrew saw more than I did in the poem. In general I agree with him. The acrostic, though, seems too easy, with nothing else providing structure to the poem.

Alice Shapiro

End of the line

Mother, whose womb I leave
to breathe
whose voice was marred
by the irony of lung disease,
I wish I had studied you.

Mother, whose womb now bereft
of sentient life
I see with blackened lungs scarred by smoke.
Fears were cloaked in disregard
and you succumbed.

While in the throes of full dependence
needing only self-satisfaction
I missed your years of sacrifice.
Your never-ending warmth
was seen as being simply mine.

This offshoot then is dedicated
to all your decency and flaws, not followed
except for fitful lapses
that last until this child arrests
the lineage, stays barren.

Critique
By Joanie DiMartino

Such a strong poem that mixes the conflict and complexities of motherhood, from the perspective of the child, looking back at birth and nursing. There is a softness to the tone, yet a distancing for the speaker, which culminates in the full detachment of the final lines, when the speaker claims ownership of childlessness.

The poem opening with, and then the later repetition of the word "Mother," serves as an invocation, and indeed the speaker is invoking the mother-figure to affirm the differences between the two; rather than bond with similarities. The line, "to all your decency and flaws, not followed" makes it clear that while the speaker acknowledges the positive aspects of child-bearing/rearing, there is a clear intent to choose a different path.

There are wonderful sounds and use of language in this short poem, which begins with the tense long "e" sound: "leave," "breathe," "disease," etc. that later turn into the long "o" sound: "smoke," "cloaked," "throes," which serves as a subtle linguistic marker delineating the change in expression of the poem, from invoking the mother to resisting her. My only suggestion to strengthen this piece would be to remove the word "simply" in line 15. This would tighten the meter, maintaining the tenseness of the language that continues to the very last line of the poem.

Reader comments

Joanna wrote:
Maybe because this piece touches me personally, having not too long ago lost my own mother to lung cancer, I really feel it is one of the strongest I have read out of the collection. I love how it transcends generations, ends with the finality of childlessness. There is a fitting melancholy to a lot of the language, and the title says so much.

Alice Shapiro

Infant, infant

It is all soft when the hand
strokes an infant's skin.
When a palm glides along its tepid surface
a blast of innate love is felt
one gets protective at the frailty of
complete dependence
exchanges depths of feeling
at first sight.

Can there be anything closer
than the stare a baby makes
in awe of discovering her mirror face?
A-gaggle at the wet tub water—
splashes, laughter, amazement!

Would that I in later years
could recall such infant scenes
instead of screams and hovering
in closets.

It is given to me
to un-remember
and to glory in the touch
of children.

Critique
By Leah Maines

The poem "Infant, infant" is as strong as a mother's bond to her child and as intricate as lace. It is graphically and sonically charged. The poet captures the images by choosing exactly the right words. In fact, I wouldn't change a thing about it. I'd happily accept it as is.

Reader comments

Sarah wrote:
Very powerful poem. The ending is unexpected, and all the more poignant for that.

Alice Shapiro

A cow woke me up

History floods a brain suddenly
upon the hearing of old tunes.
That's how this tale began
dancing to The Farmer in the Dell.

One day I woke to find myself
in grammar school
in front of the room
but centered within the group's consciousness
attached, as to a womb
with many brothers, sisters
crowding, floating round.
One droning hum of learning
that bore no quality nor distinction, no fun.

Assigned a task to draw a cow
I copied fervently and well
and was rewarded loud and hearty
which took me from the spell
of sameness.
I was now "other"
different from the rest
better, I guessed
and a hefty ego stormed.

One step further to the wall
where I was told to draw
more cows and such from memory.
I stood then on my chair
to reach the heights
of physical and mental hierarchy.

Saltian

I rose to the command, looking down
on rows of children stuck
in ordered mediocrity.
Prematurely celebrating my escape, I drew
but not a cow came through my crayoned hand.
I was drained of accuracy
alarmed at nullity
and the void where previously
I was kinged.

Shocked from sleep
into separation
into confused disappointment
I thought I was through
but shock became chagrin
as the very same admirer
who had such lengthy praise
one wide-eyed smile ago
now scolded in an angry tone.

It was too late for that
as this second birth
could not be taken back.
I would never be
an ordered row of mediocrity again
for I had witnessed self.

Alice Shapiro

Critique
By Walter Elmore

"A Cow Woke Me Up" initially reminds me of time spent in the early years of grade school where praise was easy to get from teachers and friends. You were treated special for a while because you colored inside the lines or because of your penmanship or your propensity with numbers, but like everything else, fame from such things didn't last, and soon admirers became detractors if you kept pushing your popularity. Some people get a taste of that and always want more; "[they] would never be/an ordered row of mediocrity again/for [they] had witnessed self."

On a different note, it also reminds me of the Lonely Hero archetype you see in literature and movies like, for example, the Harry Potter franchise and "The Matrix" trilogy. For example, "One day I woke to find myself/in grammar school/in front of the room/but centered within the group's consciousness ... " The Hero wakes up from the dream life he had been living, whether idyllic, abused, or ineffectual, sometimes numerous times throughout the course of the series, but they're always the object of (often unwanted) attention. Harry wakes up from the 10-year waking dream that he's a "normal" person when Hagrid shows up at the cottage on the sea to deliver his acceptance letter from Hogwarts School of Witchcraft and Wizardry. Neo wakes up from several dreams, dreams of him being implanted with a tracking device by the Agents, and waking up from the Matrix in the first film, waking up from his uncertainty of his Messianic status in the second film, and waking up from the illusion of safety and "everything will be alright" in the third film.

Saltian

"I was now 'other'/different from the rest/better, I guessed/and a hefty ego stormed." The Hero is always different, either by ability, family ties, or just by being cursed with a specific destiny. Harry and Neo are "other," which is the source of all their attention, but while Harry develops a bit of a Hero Complex without letting his ego completely storm off with him and make him into a holier-than-thou jerk, Neo remains more unsure about whether or not he actually is better than anyone, hence the " better, I guessed" line. Neither he nor Harry is really sure they're better than anyone, but Harry takes to his Chosen One destiny sooner than Neo.

Alice Shapiro

Why this, why that?

Why halt before the flame?
Why embrace the rain?
It is strange, awesome
and a wee ugly
like mud-pies and that first dirty
smoke.

The child opens up a closet door
the drawer flowered with appliqués
a white porcelain box that hides a locket.
She touches, looks, explores.

Questioning small things
that go ignored
by aged eyes and tired visions
she soaks in more, and more

becomes
the answer

Critique
By Sarah Endo

I love the description of " ... small things/that go ignored/by aged eyes and tired visions." To me, this is the beating center of the poem, providing the perfect contrast to the girl's fresh, curious eyes, and her instinct to question and explore.

I love the wonderful details, a drawer flowered with appliqués and a "white porcelain box that hides a locket"—a sphinx

wrapped in an enigma! I picture a child exploring a
grandmother's house full of beguiling antique secrets.

The opening lines of the second stanza: "It is strange, awesome/
and a wee ugly" are the most challenging part of the poem for
me. Specifically, I am not sure what "It" refers to, and if "a wee
ugly" is meant to mimic a child's diction. The rest of the poem
clearly and engagingly invites the reader into the eyes of a child.

Alice Shapiro

Miss K's arabesque

> *I go a lot to see young people downtown*
> *in little theatres. It's great. If you start*
> *somebody's career, it's so exciting.*
> —Mikhail Baryshnikov

Pink leotards, net tutus
and little girls pirouette
raise up on satin pointe shoes at the barre
arch feet and backs
stretch arms as gracefully as instructed
so poise can be constructed
into their body's consciousness.

Then onto ballet slippers
soft black leatherette with rubber band straps
to *plié, chassé, jeté*
to twirl and leap and spin at season's end recital
where fairy dancers promenade, bob and weave
in not so regimented order as perceived
and choreographed by Miss K's virtuoso desire.

Back to class, to shiny, slick parquet
a childhood filled with ballerina,
tap, toe, acrobatic antics
and all the scenes, all these years remembered.
Yet I wonder why
not once did I envision life
on stage as a dancer.

Critique
By Grace Burns

I had the honor to review "Miss K's arabesque." This poem was an absolute pleasure for me to read having been one of those little dance students in "pink leotards, net tutus" back in the seventies. "Miss K's arabesque" is multi-sensory. It conjures up the image of gaggles of girls sporting pigtails and toddler bellies in identical leotards following Miss K's instruction with round-eyed attention. Each little student believing herself every bit as graceful as Miss K. In addition, the poem's rhythm enunciates the synchronizing beat Miss K taps out while her pupils rehearse for the big recital. This is especially prevalent in the lines "arch feet and backs/stretch arms as gracefully as instructed/so poise can be constructed/into their body's consciousness."

"Yet I wonder why/not once did I envision life/on stage as a dancer." These closing lines are seemingly straightforward at first read. The author never considers becoming a professional dancer while she attended dance class as a girl. Upon reading the poem a few more times, I wonder if Ms. Shapiro is beginning to consider that life itself is a stage for her and the rest of us to dance upon. Whichever the interpretation, I have fallen in love with these lines and all the lines before it.

Reader Comments

Laughing Larry Berger wrote:
It holds to it's subject, a little too obvious for my tastes. I'd like to see a little more alliteration and less description of what actually took place. But that's me. It's a fine poem.

Alice Shapiro

Dysfunction

1.
Upon the resolution of a fight
between two adults in the clan
a child a-shiver in the corner
tries to understand
a frown or sneer
appearing on the mouth
that spews a happy word,
apologies, honor
after miscreants confuse the matter
saying one thing
harboring another.

Can you set the world aright
if ancestors mold it muddled?

2.
It is almost fun to solve a puzzle
unravel strings of life's impeccable moments
an Aha! a Wow! the
how you fit together.
And when you put a name to it
call it gone
embellish or employ it
in dance or song
the dazzle rights a wrong
sanctifies
a long-suppressed muddle.

Saltian

Critique
By Scott Owens

Coming in the Childhood section of *Saltian*, "Dysfunction" certainly captures the dynamics of a situation we, as children, commonly find ourselves in, making sense out of sarcasm. In my own experience, it seems to be something children are quite gifted at, even at very young ages, almost as if it is second nature, or instinct, for human beings to comprehend the potential for language to be duplicitous. Thus, the second stanza seems quite true, that we, even as children, relish in the understanding of sarcasm as much as in the creation of it.

As a poet, my instincts towards revising "Dysfunction" are almost entirely technical. I don't think the question that separates the two stanzas is necessary at all. It seems intrusive and untrusting of the reader's ability to apply the story being told to the world we inhabit. Additionally, I think the lines would be stronger with some changes in line breaks. The first four lines feel like trimeter to me, and I think the next line is more interesting if it continues that pattern: "a frown or a sneer appearing." There is obviously a great deal of sound play going on in the poem, and placing "sneer" and "appearing" in closer proximity further enhances that element. Continuing with this idea, I would relineate the rest of the stanza thus: "on the mouth that spews a happy / word, apologies, honor, / after miscreants confuse the matter / saying one thing harboring another." I enjoy the odd sense of "spewing a happy," the list of possibilities that follows, and the one tetrameter line coming at the end as a sort of resolution.

Alice Shapiro

Similarly, I think the final stanza becomes stronger with a relatively consistent trimeter line throughout. Doing so will deemphasize the end rhyme of "gone," "song," and "wrong," but I find such triple rhyme more effective when presented with the subtlety of internal placement. With this in mind, the stanza would be as follows:

It is almost fun to solve
a puzzle, unravel strings
of life's impeccable moments,
an Aha! a Wow! the how
you fit together. And when
you put a name to it, call it
gone, embellish or employ it
in dance or song, the dazzle
rights a wrong, sanctifies
a long-suppressed muddle.

Saltian

The sea intrudes and calms

A swim in frigid waters
whose threatening waves
dwarf a child of ten
caught by an undertow
where one's sudden breathlessness
is thrust before us
and breath's function registers valuable—
It prepares you

for death and so many death scenes
that creep into the years.

Thing is, no fear
as limbs' tension disappear
in the float
in the enveloping comfort
that is the sea
a liquid metaphor
in which the womb
resurrects.

Eyes open
peace, thoughtlessness, one.

Alice Shapiro

Critique
By KC Bosch

Alice Shapiro paints a picture here that I can see. The waves, the kid in the water and the rip currents. I have mixed emotions about this poem. I like some of the lines a lot but am troubled by others. The first stanza is very good, but seems to jump from first to second person. "and breath's function registers valuable—" is a powerful thought. And the couplet "for death and so many death scenes/that creep into the years" rings very true, but also jumps into the future before the last paragraph returns to the present. We also switch from frigid water to the enveloping comfort of the sea. Overall the idea of drowning being peaceful and free from fear is troubling.

Saltian

The Feast of St. Catherine

Our carnival at the vacant lot
burst onto town each June
like a Verdi opera.
Pink gossamer to eat
mud-stomped grass beneath our feet
a shrill Italian song
emanating over children's jeers
the aim to win
to beat old carnys' sleights
against all odds.

And the gambler's vice begins.

Day fades, lanterns light
a crowd wanders, circling
tent-booths lined with wooden ducks
dead to barrels
aimed to kill.

And the gun for sport dawns.

We spin around on giant teacups
dizzy from the ride
take note of a faint, free mind

and reach for sweet, indulgent wine.

Alice Shapiro

At dusk, painted horses gallop on their everlasting turns
help us grab the golden ring
and if our sense is strong enough

a holy promise sings.

Critique: Responsive Writing Aimed to Kill
By Maxwell Baumbach

it doesn't last

spin in those giant teacups
before the holy promiser
picks them up and eats them
like Willy Wonka did in the room
of edible treats

it's good to see you realize
days are fading

soon your dreams will
too

don't keep reaching for the golden ring

the only thing that will result from it
is a torn rotator cuff

Saltian

promises are no different than hearts

made to be broken
or at least abused

one of a holy nature
only assures hypocrisy

the barrels are aimed to kill
what you hope will be born
tomorrow

Alice Shapiro

Sex

A summer bungalow arouses secret lusts
as sunbeams peek through tattered curtains
and a three-year-old, crumpled under cotton covers
titters at her father's work-mate's muscles
and sun-bronzed arms that taunt and tickle her.
Desire forms and a sense of future
different than the entertaining toy
or a parent's unconditional comfort.

One day in a grown time
this same woman knelt to weed a garden.
A shadow blocked her light
as two bright eyes
peered down.
The neighbor's son at seven
silent and enticed
flowered.

Critique: Responsive Writing
Sex
By Bryan Borland

> *The parents, denying it in themselves,*
> *were horrified to find it in their children.*
> —John Steinbeck, from *East of Eden*

He discovered his body in the bathtub,
toy ships bobbing with tides of pulling and prodding
in company of rose-faced others who refused

to acknowledge how the arch of the sun
can touch a child's skin in the early dawn.
It is the shameful unspoken,
schooled out like fantasies of girls
in red cloaks or ginger-laced gluttony.

When the wolves bayed at fourteen
and were allowed in again, his eyes drifted
past the childhood relic:
a yellow boat, at peace
on a shelf warmed
by natural light;
his mid-morning
heat.

Reader comments

Jean wrote:
With regard to the poem, "Sex," I am attempting to contain my disgust. Having spent my professional life working to protect children from sexual abuse and its effects with different levels of success, I find prurience, disguised as art, repugnant.

Stan wrote:
Wow. I understand Jean's comment out of context. I did not read the poem the same way. I read nothing in the adult characters that would suggest that they are aware of anything sexual in the two scenarios. Rather, I think Alice is suggesting that there are subliminal cues that much later become sexual but cannot be processed that way by the children. The title, then, may be what

Alice Shapiro

is offensive in the poem rather than the content. A different title, say "Beginning Adulthood" or "Silent Seeds" or some such might get the same idea across with less offense for some readers. Just my thoughts at the moment.

Rae Spencer wrote:
I find this poem offensive. The following is not meant to be an instruction on how the poem should be read, simply an explanation of my own reading.

For me, failure begins with the poem's title and placement in the manuscript. Why "Sex"? Especially in a section devoted to "Childhood"? This poses an immediate obstacle, and I now approach the poem with a sense of dread. A different title would set the stage differently, although changing the title will not salvage the poem.

The first line, which is the poem's first opportunity to deny the more sinister aspects of its title, sets the scene in a "summer bungalow," uses the verb "arouses," and directs the reader's attention to "secret lusts." This is the language of romance novels, grossly misplaced in a section titled "Childhood."

The poem turns even more grotesque when it writes a three-year-old girl into this setting and places her in bed with an adult man. The child "titters at her father's work-mate's muscles/and sun-bronzed arms that taunt and tickle her."

Why emphasize the man's "sun-bronzed arms"? Why, in a poem otherwise devoid of physical description, is it important to describe the man's bare skin? And why, with such a wealth of words to choose from, am I told that the child "titters"? Given the poem's other purposeful references to sex, the rude term hidden in the word's syllables seems equally purposeful. Why use the phrase "work-mate"? How about "coworker"? Instead, the child is in bed with a "mate." An accumulation of sexual language, leading up to the suggestion that the girl experiences "desire." By this point, I am thoroughly appalled.

The second stanza is less flagrant, but the first stanza has already set the tone. Again, a child is "enticed" toward sexual maturity by an adult.

Part of the poem's failure is its inability to defy alternate readings. Ms. Shapiro must have been aware that readers might perceive the scenes as unwholesome. But the poem does not offer any guidance for interpretation. It does not address any moral implications. It proceeds as if unaware that interactions between children and adults are sometimes monstrously abusive, as if it should be immune from comparison with such monstrosities.

An argument to counter my reading is as follows: if I find something unwholesome in these scenes, then I must be borrowing from an experience outside the poem. I might concede the point, if the poem's topic was a less dangerous one, if there were fewer harrowing experiences to borrow. In my opinion, when a poem presumes to describe children in sexual language, it must acknowledge that such descriptions are

Alice Shapiro

potentially predatory. At a minimum, it must address the conflict such descriptions pose for a reader, and for the world. Failure to do so renders the poem utterly useless to me. Up to this point, I have been happy to add my voice to WIP: *Saltian*. However, I cannot support the publication of this poem.

Ray Sharp wrote:
This poem confuses me for a different reason. The first section is in the present tense—arouses, titters, forms. Then in the latter section, the poet switches to past tense—knelt, blocked, peered, flowered. But it seems that the 3-year-old is now the same woman "in a grown time." Am I reading this right? The present tense is used when she was 3, then past tense when she was an adult? Is there some mysterious reversal of time, because the first part in the present tense makes us think it is happening now, and the second section seems a remembered scene? Or are they different people, poetically called "this same woman" as if we are talking about an archetype, not the actual same person? Hmmm ... now I'm really confused. I understood the construction to mean that it was the same person, with role reversal, first the innocent feeling her first vague stirring of sexuality, and then later, the object of such feelings. I do not say the "cause" of the sexual awakening, just the "object," because I am not convinced that the adults in this poem are provocateurs. I did not read that the man was in bed with the girl. As I read it, I thought the girl was under the covers, perhaps remembering an encounter with the man, but not necessarily an improper one. I would agree that this is a sensitive subject, and some ambiguities in the text could provoke strong feelings. For that reason, I

Saltian

would recommend a re-write. Not because poems need to explain everything, but because in this case I think some poor phrasing is leading the reader astray from the poet's intended subject into very distracting places.

Joanna wrote:
First let me say congratulations to Ms. Shapiro. It takes good poetry to bring out such strong responses; good poetry polarizes — good poetry makes you feel deep down in your guts.

Clearly there is something of value here then. From Bryan's (a poet of no mean reputation himself, in my humble opinion) glowing response, to Rae and Jean's (two women for whom I have tremendous respect as writers) vehement rebuttals. There must be more than one way to read this piece, and, from the good bit I've experienced so far from Ms. Shapiro's *Saltian*, I find it hard to believe that her intention was to repulse readers with favorable descriptions of childhood abuse.

To me, on first read, what this poem addresses is the awareness of sexual possibility. The three-year-old is seeing in her father's companion the woman she might become—not in the sense of sharing his bed, but rather in the feminine shape with developed muscles and curves which will some day be hers. It's an alluring possibility, even to a child of three. Then we see the same child, grown, now an object of desire herself to a seven-year-old boy who is obviously dealing with his own confused ideas about adulthood and sex.

Alice Shapiro

I agree with Jean and Rae that some of the language can be misleading—more overtly sexual than childlike—in a way possibly Ms. Shapiro did not intend. I can see how the title can be misconstrued, and I like Stan's suggestions of something less outright ... maybe "Seeds," or "Beginnings." Words like "taunt" and "enticed" also strike me as possibly too adult-ly sexual for a poem about childhood.

On a side note, I very much like the way Bryan gives his own interpretation on the same theme, and I think he does so successfully, nodding to the *verboten* nature of the topic in passing, and not apologizing for it. I don't think Ms. Shapiro should, either, but merely clarify with her language the images she means to convey.

Annmarie wrote:

As a late comment to this thread I'm posting Alice's revised poem, now titled "Seeds," as it will appear in the book.

Seeds

A summer bungalow awakes
as sunbeams peek through tattered curtains
and a three-year-old, crumpled under cotton covers
giggles at the friend her father introduces
as his sun-bronzed, muscled arms tickle her.
Desire forms and a sense of future
different than the entertaining toy
or a parent's unconditional comfort.

Saltian

One day in a grown time
this same woman kneels to weed a garden.
A shadow blocks her light.
She turns, looks up
as two bright eyes peer down.
The neighbor's son at seven
silent and awakened
flowers.

Rae Spencer wrote:
With the revisions, I no longer find the poem so blazingly offensive, though I still believe its content is ill-advised. My objection hinges on the poem's insistence that awakenings of sexuality in children are catalyzed by adult interaction—by "sun-bronzed, muscled arms" and a woman kneeling in a garden. For me, the scenes are not unique enough, the language is not fresh enough, and the meter, rhyme, and rhythm are not rich enough to overcome the poem's dangerous assertions regarding the role of adults in a child's journey of self-discovery.

Summer bungalows and sunbeams, tattered curtains and cotton covers are pretty images, but they fall into the realm of cliche unless described in new terms that bring a new perspective to such scenery. The word "crumpled" is an interesting choice, but I find its use unfortunate as it highlights the helplessness of a three-year-old child. The child is tickled by "sun-bronzed, muscled arms," but it is unclear whether the arms belong to the friend or the father. Then I am told that "desire forms." Am I to read here that the three-year-old experiences sexual desire brought on by the sight of an adult's muscles, by an adult's touch? Is that adult her father's friend or her father?

Alice Shapiro

In the second stanza, the girl is grown to adulthood. She is placed, once more, in a vulnerable position—kneeling in a garden. Here again, I do not find enough music in the lines. Verb choice is plain ("blocks," "turns," "looks," "peer") and there are no details to enrich the scene. The stanza is entirely dependent on the last word, "flowers." Am I to understand that the boy exposes himself to the woman? That a 7-year-old boy experiences sexual arousal at the sight of a woman kneeling in a garden?

Unanswered questions are not failures in poetry, but in this case the questions approach dangerous thresholds. Even this might be acceptable if the negative aspects of the poem were balanced by outstanding merit in construction, but in "Seeds," I do not feel the poem is worth its price.

One further note: Mr. Borland's response poem is a useful contrast to "Seeds." For me, "Sex" succeeds where "Seeds" fails: it introduces a narrative about conflict (framed by the opening quotation), takes a stand regarding that narrative, and challenges me to consider my own stand. Most significantly, it provides a narrative of childhood self-discovery that is independent of adult provocation. In fact, the adults of this poem are remote and disapproving, with their "rose-faced" denial and rejection of the "shameful unspoken." Additionally, the poem is lyrically strong in its focus on the toy boat and sun, which age alongside the boy; in its use of unique and interesting phrases ("ginger-laced gluttony," "the wolves bayed again at fourteen," "childhood relic"); and with its final abatement of conflict mediated by words like "peace," "warmed," and "natural light."

Saltian

In the morning, looking

Cut from a family's cord
a first sweet lust-experiment
may last a mind's lifetime
despite a ruptured covenant.

Her adoration
swept up at the flush
of a warm cheek
steals her attention
as she traces every line
studies with enchanted eyes
every muscle-bulge on a lover's thigh.

This is not scrutiny.
It is an amorous regard
without a drop of prejudice
no preference
a wonderment at custody
of love.

Critique
By Joanna S Lee

"In the morning, looking" paints a still-life capturing the dew-fresh memories of first love. The poem serves nicely as an introduction to the "Lover" section of *Saltian*; it fairly brims not only with physical love and lust, but with the youthful optimism of a first time at either. There is much of both a literal and a metaphorical "morning" in language and in tone.

Alice Shapiro

While I'm a big fan of the way Ms. Shapiro breaks up both lines and verses here, giving the reader little pauses to let each image sink in, I do think the flow of the piece could be improved upon a little, especially in the final verse, where a scarcity of punctuation left me unsure of how to read those last several lines.

I also love how the line "Her adoration" stands alone, drawing emphasis not only to whomever "she" is as the subject of the poem, but also to the young, positive feel of the piece overall. The lines that follow, though, could possibly be made to flow a little more smoothly with the slightest of tweaks, as, for one example:

> Her adoration
>
> is swept up at the flush
> of a warm cheek,
> her attention stolen
> as she traces every line,
> ...

As Ms. Shapiro herself says, "[t]his is not scrutiny." Rather, these are merely tiny suggestions to what is regardless a delightfully sweet and poignant read.

Saltian

Catching love

> *Happiness is a butterfly, which when*
> *pursued, is always just beyond your*
> *grasp, but which if you will sit down*
> *quietly, may alight upon you.*
> —Nathaniel Hawthorne

Malaysian stew, too oily for enjoyment
is pushed aside.
She leaves the table
and the day—rain cannot stop her plan.

With great speed
she organizes artistic work in sections
labels, stacks, orders drawings
but the shelf stays sweeter than sweated-over painted dreams.

Mid-life, mid-career
this frantic phase spans years
long away from him
and a peace once afforded two.

To think about the battle
to change from human love to hobby love
one wonders after having lost them both
which love is best to hunt?

Too young to sift though
a gold-weave basket of inherited traits
too old to labor for elusive truth
the ocean-tossed decade
stays a cache of passionate yearning.

Alice Shapiro

Critique
By Ray Sharp

Sister Poet, they seated us at this small round table at the edge of the crowded dance floor, knee to knee so that we both see the whirl of shadow dancers. They know we are alike, two poets in their middle years, too wise or just too damn tired for chasing love. You place before us the apple (the French *pomme* and the English *poem*, fruits of different roots, but entwined branches?) and gesture for me to pick up the knife. I cleave the shiny red thing to expose its white flesh and five-chambered heart. You arrange between us the five dark seeds, and I take each in turn, and chew and swallow their bitter truths:

The first stanza is for setting the scene. Who has not pushed aside the oily stew and fled alone into hard rain? I hear the tropical downpour drum so loudly on the tin roofs that it's hard to think, so you just react. Your madras dress is soaked through but there is no relief from the steamy midday heat.

The second stanza sweeps us up into the action, the pace, and we are running to keep up with the poet who is running for her life.

The third stanza connects the immediacy of the present tense with the bigger story to be told. It is her story, so we think of our own stories, each unique and yet every one the same.

Saltian

Everything hinges on the problematic fourth stanza. These are the questions that haunt us as we pivot from past to future, young to old. And yet, the poet has chosen the impersonal—archaic?—"one" as the subject. It is a matter of meaning and also of style. Another poet might have said "she wonders" referring to the protagonist from the opening lines. Or "you," the modern form of "one" which this poet uses to connect the poem to the reader and vice versa. Or "I." Each word we choose makes a different poem.

The fifth stanza, full of poetry—traits/truths, cache of/passion. This stanza has five lines instead of four. Why? Because the last line gives us closure, resolution, as much sense as we, or she, or you, can make of that stormy period between young and old.

Alice Shapiro

Where is the love?
By Alice Shapiro

> *I think art education, especially*
> *in this country, which government*
> *pretty much ignores, is so important*
> *for young people.*
> —Mikhail Baryshnikov

Morning's drift puts him off
as dreams grasp at waking layers
pull and push
sleepy eyes
retreat and reluctance.

Endeav'ring to fulfill
a father's plan
follow the design demanded
before being born
he wilts like old cabbage leaves
unfit for sweet crunchy slaw.

> To put a foot out the door
> he drags his attitude forward
> claws his way to fortune
> ignoring gnawing taps upon
> a half-accomplished dance career.

Years shall pass
he may forget his passion
while wrapped in cuddled levels of temporary love.

Saltian

Side-tracked, extracting what's expected
all strength drained and waning
will he have time instead to overthrow traditions?

Critique
By Jim Valvis

1. Title
 Where is the love?

I'm not sure of the purpose of this title. Doesn't seem to add much and doesn't do much to lead us into the poem. I don't think "love" is the right word here anyway. I think you really mean "passion." This is especially true given you make the distinction between "passion" and "temporary love" in the final stanza.

2. Quote
> *I think art education, especially*
> *in this country, which government*
> *pretty much ignores, is so important*
> *for young people.*
> —Mikhail Baryshnikov

This is simply too long. It's practically an essay before you enter the poem. The quote is very prosaic, artless. Though I've done so myself, I'm not a big fan of this kind of attribution, but if it must be done, let it be as short and pointed as possible, especially when you're not dealing with lines of verse. Furthermore, I'm bothered by the political message. It's not an overtly political poem, doesn't deal with art education, or the government. Frankly, I'd either cut the whole business, find a way to rewrite the poem so that the quote becomes obligatory, or move it into the title somehow. If it must be there, cut it to the quick:

> [A]rt education... is so important for young people.
> —Mikhail Baryshnikov

3. Verse 1
Morning's drift puts him off
as dreams grasp at waking layers
pull and push
sleepy eyes
retreat and reluctance.

First of all, I'm not entirely sure what this means. Are you trying to describe a man stumbling from bed or a man frustrated by circumstances or both? Whatever the case, it needs work. Think clarity. If you're able, try to use concrete and sensual details, but if you must—simply tell us what you mean. Ted Kooser says the beginning of a poem is where clarity matters most. You want to invite the reader inside the poem and make him comfortable. By comfortable, he does not mean calm or lacking tension, but grounded and knowing his footing.

Anyway, just going by what's here, I will say you have a nice run of opposites with dreams/waking layers and pull/push, but you start to lose it with sleepy eyes (cliche) and then lose it completely with retreat/reluctance, which are not opposites or even at odds with each other. The "sleepy eyes" bothers me in its placement anyway. If you're going to keep it, and not change it for something stronger, I suggest moving it away from the opposites.

Morning's drift puts him off
sleepy eyes
as dreams grasp at waking layers
pull and push
retreat and reluctance.

Better, but better still would be "retreat and advance." Isn't there a dance step of forward and back you could call on?

Finally, the lack of punctuation does not bother me, except that in the final stanza a comma suddenly appears. Either you're going to use commas in the poem, or line breaks as commas, or you are not. Like Mr. Miyagi says, "You karate do yes, okay. You karate do no, okay. You karate do 'guess so,' squish like grape." Well, you punctuation do yes or no, but you punctuation do sometimes, squishy poet.

4. Verse 2
Endeav'ring to fulfill
a father's plan
follow the design demanded
before being born
he wilts like old cabbage leaves
unfit for sweet crunchy slaw.

Alice Shapiro

What is the purpose of ruining the word "endeavoring"? Are you endeavoring to destroy your poem? Listen, the reason poets used to truncate the syllables in words, like "o'er the land of the free," was so they could keep the meter right—especially when poetry was mainly sung or performed, rather than read on a page. This is not a metered poem, and its primary audience consists of readers. Doing something like this makes the poet look like a rank amateur. Worse, it pulls the reader out of the poem to figure out why an apostrophe is sitting in the middle of a word. I'm not one for making a lot of rules, but unless you're playing it for laughs, or writing old-fashioned sonnets, you should never do this.

Why is it "a father's plan," emphasis on the indefinite article? Is it any old father? Or is it his father?

I don't care for "before being born," when just "before born" or "before birth" will do. But if it was up to me I would just drop it all. A father's plans for his kid always predate the kid's own plans. We get it.

I like a lot "he wilts like old cabbage leaves." I just don't know if it belongs in this poem. It's the only garden/vegetable image. It comes out of nowhere and disappears into nothing. You would think there would be some kind of art/dance/ballet image here, but instead we're talking about cabbage and a KFC side dish. I do not like the "sweet crunchy slaw" here anyway, since the idea is that he is entering a world where he doesn't belong and that is somehow less than the artistic world he should be entering, so why is that world sweet and crunchy? Or perhaps you mean the dance world is sweet and crunchy? Well, it's not clear. But even if that's the case, the image just doesn't work in this context. Why not just have him grow fat?

5. Verse 3
To put a foot out the door
he drags his attitude forward
claws his way to fortune
ignoring gnawing taps upon
a half-accomplished dance career.

Clearly the best stanza in the poem. The mentions of "foot" and "taps" have nice dance overtones. A couple of issues, though. I see no reason why this stanza should be tabbed out differently than the others. It seems merely random and random formatting in poetry is almost as bad as mutilating words when it comes to distracting the reader. He asks himself, why is the author doing this? If he doesn't reach a clear answer soon, he grows confused and the poem suffers. Also, I wasn't sure about the word "claws," especially since it seems too clever with the aw-aw-aw with "ignoring gnawing," especially since claws, again, has nothing to do with the arts/dance. However, the one I disliked most was "half-accomplished." It's both a mouthful and needlessly prosaic. Pull out the thesaurus and find something better. Unrealized. Abridged. Unconsummated. Almost anything else. I'd also take a close look at the word "career." Isn't the whole point of the poem that dance is a passion and more than just a career?

You should question every word in this manner.

Alice Shapiro

6. Final Stanza
Years shall pass
he may forget his passion
while wrapped in cuddled levels of temporary love.
Side-tracked, extracting what's expected
all strength drained and waning
will he have time instead to overthrow traditions?

Shall and may don't work. Shall is old fashioned and unneeded. May is a word that lacks conviction. Isn't the tragedy that he loses his connection with dance? You're writing a tragedy here, so write a tragedy. Have the courage to stick with it. After all, it's not the character you're trying to steer toward your point of view, it's the reader.

Years pass
he forgets his passion

The next line is too long for the poem. "Cuddled levels" doesn't work and isn't needed. Omit.

wrapped in temporary love.

We already know he's side-tracked, the whole poem has been telling us that. Omit.

Extracting what's expected

Strength cannot be "drained and waning." If strength is drained, he has none. A drained sink has no water. The water cannot

Saltian

therefore also be waning. It can be draining and waning, but the rhyme, I fear, would be too much—and it would be redundant, not to mention mixing water and light images. Again it would be so much better if there was a dance verb here, but sticking with what you have in place:

strength waning

In my opinion, the first and last lines are the most important in the poem. Let's look at your last.

will he have time instead to overthrow traditions?

Up till now, you've given us no reason to think he will, so why ask the question? Again, you're writing a tragedy, but you don't seem to want to let it be a tragedy. Let it be a tragedy. A poem is only as strong as the author behind it has conviction. With that in mind, the poem would be much more powerful if you don't leave the question open at the end, but instead bring the man to defeat with something like:

he tumbles toward tradition.

See what I've done? I've used a negative dance image—tumbles—to show the tragedy. He's no dancer, he's followed the wishes of his father.

The last stanza, then, might look something like this:

Alice Shapiro

Years pass.
he forgets his passion,
wrapped in temporary love.
Extracting what's expected,
strength waning,
he tumbles toward tradition.

Alice, as you can see, I'm a tough critic, but only because I think you have a good poem here that hasn't yet realized its full potential. I hope something I said helps. If nothing else, if only you don't mutilate the word endeavoring, you'll have made this a stronger poem.

Reader comments

Jean wrote:
Mr. Valvis' critique, while comprehensive, is verbose, and could profit from editing and fewer clever remarks.

Saltian

The transparency of a Spanish fly

In Acapulco
ten years after
a loosed marriage-bed
she sat alone at the edge
of a flowery-patterned sofa
reverie interrupted
when a younger pair took
the other cushion
unaware of her presence.

> Cooing like a cockatiel in heat
> the sexy lady rambled on
> with a Castilian beat
> talking up what seemed
> ordinary speak.

Being peripheral and non-existent
she observed with blatant courage
their love-dance.

> He begged, he pleaded
> his question unheeded
> and her bleating chatter
> bleeding on his persistence.

Neither woman budged.
The hot sun went down.

Alice Shapiro

At the same moment they both knew
his infant frown and escalating ardor
must be caught
like a fly in a sticky viscid trap.

        She picked the ripe-ready fruit
        and with an imperceptible smile
        it was over.
        They left the couch
        hand in hand.
        An elevator took them up
        doors closed on hasty exploration.

The lesson came too late.

Critique
By Stan Galloway

The title allows for several possibilities. Before reading the poem, a reader will likely think of the aphrodisiacal version of Spanish fly, which works in the poem, as the sexual ardor is documented, possibly for all three of the people present. The fact that the difference between efficacy and toxicity in a dose of Spanish fly is quite narrow shows the fine line between success and failure between the two women in the poem. But the use of the indefinite article "a" in the title would indicate a second meaning. The setting in Acapulco is Spanish and the unnamed woman at the beginning of the poem is settled in the flowers (of the sofa) just watching, unnoticed, a "fly on the wall." She becomes "a Spanish fly." Likewise the word "transparency" carries double interpretation, first as in "obvious or evident" and the second as "looked through or unseen." In this regard the title is well-formed.

The form of the poem also carries several significant characteristics. The seven sections of the poem serve as a subtle reminder of the book's seven-part structure (though these sections do not mirror the seven categories). The alternating point of view is visible structurally with the older woman's view flush left and the younger couple's focus in the indented stanzas. This structure makes it clear that the final line is from the older woman's point of view. The line is a bit puzzling. Was it that she has just been given a lesson on how to get a man to her bed (ten years after her marriage has ended) and she deems herself "too late" to play that game? Or is the lesson, given some of the diction analysis below, about the pitfalls of sex, which she learned through her own negative experience, making this lesson "too late"? Or, if one ignores the structural cue, could the lesson be the man's inability to see the trap that he's been drawn into? I assume this from the woman's femininity being described as "a sticky viscid trap." But in stanza 4, he is the one begging and pleading, which makes him both pursuer and victim. While ambiguity can enhance a poem, the uncertainty with the final line, leaves me more confused than enriched.

The poem, as a narrative, is evocative, though the words in some places seem ill-fitting. The rhyme, both end-line and internal, seems random, drawing attention to itself without emphasizing

Alice Shapiro

key words. In this case, unless I've overlooked some other significance, the effort not to rhyme might be worthwhile. Some specific words that seem close to the right word, but not, are "flowery" instead of "flower" in stanza 1, "speak" instead of "speech" in stanza 2, and "ripe-ready" instead of one or the other but not both in stanza 6. But the effective use of words is far more common. My vote for best phrase in the poem goes to the end of stanza 4: "her bleating chatter/bleeding on his persistence." The image of her words flowing liquidly over his incorporeal persistence is both surreal and sensual. The penultimate line, also well-worded—"doors closed on hasty exploration"—is suggestive without being prurient. The poem is neither simple nor obscure, though some fine-tuning of diction may make a good poem even better.

Jealous plate

Alone, under an umbrella'd bistro
wild geese passing by
I peered skyward and backward.
Why?

It was a plea from once-kissed lips ...

Where is the absent occupant
whose chair should be energized
with laughs and conversation
exchanging giddy romances?

The prize escaped, dining elsewhere.

Dinner came
arranged luxuriously on heated china.
I ate politely
thinking hate.

Her arms entangled round his wrist.

Pretzel-twisted feelings rose
accompanied by my swallow-gulps
of undigested Bourbon shrimp.
I drowned in angered waters

cursed Fate.

Alice Shapiro

Critique
By Jean McLeod

I loved this poem. While of a serious nature, there appears to be an undercurrent of humor that gives it even more charm. The subject matter, lost love, is universal, with the feeling of jealousy and the surety that one will die making it compelling. The arrangement of stanzas, four lines followed by one line, is rhythmic, pleasing in sound and on the page.

The first stanza begins in the first person past tense, while the third changes to first person present. The author may have done this purposefully. Also, the third stanza addresses the chair, rather than a person. It might be more effective to speak of a "love" or "lover" than an inanimate object and to choose a more personal verb in the second line than "energize." Again, in the third stanza, "Exchanging giddy romances" seems a little forced, and might be a place to study. The fourth stanza returns to past tense.

The denouement "I drowned in angered waters/Cursed Fate" is effective for placement on the page and for the ambiguity—did she REALLY, or did she WANT to drown??? GOOD SHOW! Thanks for a great ride!

Observations:
Jealous plate   *Great title*

Alone, under ~~an~~ umbrella'd bistro	*a bit of a tongue-twister with all of the "a"s*
wild geese passing by	
I peered skyward, ~~and~~ backward.	*Beautiful!*
Why?	

Saltian

~~It was~~ A plea from once-kissed lips; *changes from past tense to present. Is this purposeful?*

Where is *(was?)* my absent love *"love" seems more to the point than "occupant"*

whose ~~chair~~ presence should enchant
~~be energized~~   *perhaps concentrate on the person not the chair?*

with laughter and conversation
the exchange of giddy glance? ~~romances?~~

The prize escaped, dined elsewhere.   *back to past tense; I'm pretty sure it's on purpose*

Dinner came
~~arranged~~ luxurious~~ly~~ on heated china.
I ate politely
thinking hate.

Her arms entangled round his wrist.   *Love this!*

Pretzel-twisted feelings rose
accompanied by my swallow-gulps
of undigested Bourbon shrimp.
I drowned in angered waters

cursed Fate.

Alice Shapiro

For efficacy, and only that, since I do not expect Alice to adopt all or, indeed, any of these observations, this is what the poem would look like if they were put into effect without comments:

Jealous plate

Alone, under umbrella'd bistro
wild geese passing by
I peered skyward, backward.
Why?

A plea from once-kissed lips:

Where is my absent love
whose presence should enchant
with laughter and conversation

the exchange of giddy glance?

The prize escaped, dined elsewhere.

Dinner came
luxurious on heated china.
I ate politely
thinking hate.

Her arms entangled round his wrist.
Pretzel-twisted feelings rose
accompanied by my swallow-gulps

of undigested Bourbon shrimp.
I drowned in angered waters

cursed Fate.

Reader comments

Stan wrote:
While Jean has given not only suggestions but reasons for the suggestions, I will quibble over the use of "chair" in line 7. I think the shift from the absent person to the chair works to move to something concrete rather than the absence, and in doing so emphasizes the absence, because the person is NOT there, but the chair is. I recommend keeping the chair (even empty).

Jean wrote:
Thank you for your opinion, Stan, I think it makes excellent sense and seems not a quibble at all.

Jean wrote:
On the other hand, could the chair be energized "with laughs and conversation/giddy romances..."
or would that phrase, perhaps, likely modify, "Where is my the absent occupant..."(a cold word when speaking of a past love, in my opinion) which still points out the lack of occupant.

I think a case might be made for your point or for mine. In either case, it depends upon the author's intent and voice, and clearly, you are right in defending the author's wording.

Alice Shapiro

The salve of women meeting

I came
anticipated
ate and drank.

We entered into lively chats
laughed and cried
bonded.

Women in the field
in the depth of
ascension

business, business done
profit by embracing wisdom
in a similar realm.

Support, comfort
shared adventures
and we glide through silt

sludge, sediment,
and help quash tattered worn-out theories
exhale, stroke the sun.

Spinning, Spinning, and Then Lifting: A Response to Alice Shapiro's "The salve of women meeting"
By KJ Hannah Greenberg

Wise, crone poet, Alice Shapiro, writes in "The salve of women meeting" about we women's ability to unite to lift ourselves

Saltian

above seemingly crushing problems. Her text shows readers that by applying coordinated effort, we can pull ourselves up to otherwise unimagined levels of self-worth.

Set in her book, *Saltian*, which is rubriced in keeping with the Seven Ages of Man, as explicated by William Shakespeare, in his play, *As You Like It*, "The salve of women meeting" describes how the author and her cohorts, allegedly assembled to engage in a career-related *ballabile*, actually draw closer in their pacifying of each other over their respective partners' offstage behaviors. That is, upon losing their communication inhibitions, this poem's daughters neither moan nor scream about their common troubles, but chat about shared solutions. They proffer comfort and support to each other as they glide through all too familiar "silt, slush [and] sediment" and then conclude their congress with a supernatural *échappé sauté*, which boosts them high enough to reach a celestial body, ie, to "stroke the sun."

Interestingly, despite the fact that "The salve of women meeting" falls into *Saltian*'s third section, into that passage of life Shakespeare assigned to The Lover[1], to unbridled passion accompanied by delusional mentations concerning life's relative ease, Shapiro's resourceful players suffer no hysterics, gender notwithstanding, when their days and nights prove to be challenge-filled. Rather than acquiescing to fervor, this poem's protagonists cast off of unnecessary accountability, per se, in the process of their self-elevation; they feel no compunction to ape their dear ones' obsessions.

Alice Shapiro

Whether the men in these women's lives are demanding perfect, three-minute eggs, or are insisting on intimacies more exotic than those of the Kama Sutra, we can't know. Looking between the lines, though, we can deduce that those invisible counterparts will continue to low like cattle whether they are stuck without recipes or caught between the sheets while their women stride forward. Sure Shapiro's gals do cry, perhaps from relief in having found kindred spirits, or perhaps from exhaustion in having carried their relational toxics alone for too long, but those females, as well, "quash [their men's] worn-out theories" and elsewise get over limiting ideations that are too unrealistic to put into good practice.

Shapiro's careful word choice and her attention to her phrases' telegraphy enable her to convey those teachings. In "The salve of women meeting's" fourth stanza, for instance, the poet repeats the word "business," as an evocation both of a dance's minced steps and as a reinforcement of the notion that the busy work, particular to women's ways, is an entrepreneurship all its own.

Similarly, Shapiro's avatar performs solo in "The salve of women meeting's" first stanza, but interacts with the entire *troupe de danse* in the rest of the poem. It is as though, through this placement of characters, the author is reminding us that whereas we can find our answers among friends, we come, by ourselves, to our private states of affairs, and depart from them alone.

What's more, in this piece's closing stanza, a magnificent finale occurs. The sun is invited to take the stage as a *danseur nobel*, as the primary ballerino, as a singular counterpoint to an entire band of women, whose adventures were, until that moment, better served without any embodiment of masculinity. As such, the literal star beckons hope and summons the possibility of reconfigured optimism in the intimate lives of the narrator and of her associates.

"The salve of women meeting" shows that we maidens, mothers, matrons, mistresses all, seek balm for the ills of our times and shows that we can discover emotional unguent in each other's company. This poem also introduces the makings for arriving at peace with our lovers and for enjoying romantic exchanges without losing our integrity.

It is hard to justify running from our worries, whether we try to escape in small *développés* or in *grandes jetés* when such good advice is available. "The salve of women meeting" is a poem worth reading.

1. "And then the lover, / Sighing like furnace, with a woeful ballad / Made to his mistress' eyebrow." William Shakespeare. *As You Like It*. 2/7.

Reader comments

Alice Wells wrote:
Very deep! I hope to read this one again and looking forward to more.

Alice Shapiro

Carlene Tejada wrote:
This is a thoughtful interpretation of "The salve of women meeting." Among other connections in Greenberg's critique, I particularly enjoyed her comments on the relationship of the poem to *Saltian*, the book. However, the FIRST response to the FIRST poem in this project could have been less academic with fewer unfamiliar words and French phrases without translation. Such scholarly approaches, though useful in a university classroom, scare hopefuls from opening a poetry book or picking up a pen to write and submit their own poems for publication.

Florence Joffe wrote:
After reading Ms.Shapiro's last two books, *Cracked* and *Life*, I am convinced she is an esoteric poet. At first I could not understand where she was coming from, but reading it the second time and coming to the last line "stroke the sun" it all came together. This is what happens in most of her poems. It's her trademark Whatever the subject, you will find a phrase, sentence or word that pulls it all together. This is what fascinates about her poetry.

Alice Wells wrote:
Oh, I agree.

Jean McLeod wrote:
I thoroughly enjoyed this poem; felt it accessible to women who gather in groups and find support. Ms. Greenberg's critique shows a marvelous grasp of the academic, but seems to go somewhat beyond the information inherent in either Ms. Shapiro's poem or Shakespeare's The Seven Ages of Man. Its 10 paragraphs exceeded the prescribed instructions of 3 paragraphs by more than the power of 3. I longed to incorporate more in a critique, but attempted to stay within guidelines.

Saltian

Desire

> *A friend is a second self*
> —Aristotle

> *The cries of Lois*
> *the dearth of shame*
> *the help of brothers*
> *the force of disdain*
> *the books of poets*
> *the poems of rain*
> —Alice Shapiro, post meridiem

I cannot tell whether
diamonds appeared in *his* eyes
or mine
as the shine of adoration
became the icon
one values in history
a Byzantine sparkle
Medieval armor against all odds.

We stand on stages
act our play
sometimes alone in our heads
    (before the mating)
sometimes in platitudes and lies
    (after years together).
I recognize the dew
and the frost.

Alice Shapiro

Can you come to me innocent
each day, each moment
where a diamond's glint
appears as highlights
between your words
between our silences
as we lie down
in fields of smiles?

Critique
By Harrison Solow

"Betwixt" is the figure that appears most prominently in what seems at times a lament, at times an abbreviated Song of Songs, that ultimate chronicle of Desire, in Alice Shapiro's poem of the same name. The use of the word, betwixt, rather than "between" is deliberate, both as a symbol and a reference.

Symbolically, the word stands for the space between the words and silences, between the frost and the dew, between the stage and the performer, as perceived by the speaker. Betwixt is what lies between the I and Thou in these stanzas, both as barrier and corridor, almost another voice in the cry for connection.

As a reference, this wedged word harks back to Shakespeare's time, when its use was common, and specifically to his Sonnet 47, of which an echo (of the first line) is heard in Ms. Shapiro's poem above:

Saltian

"Betwixt mine eye and heart a league is took,
And each doth good turns now unto the other:
When that mine eye is famish'd for a look,
Or heart in love with sighs himself doth smother ..."

Desire is dichotomous poem—of uncertainty and distance in relational tension with (or to) its own desire and attachment. It affords a richness of speculation and a palette of questions. If I were to make an emendation, it would be to remove the italics from the second line and find an alternative for "our values" which has become a stock phrase in political campaigns and rather jars with the dreamy, speculative nature inherent in the poet's elegiac questions of art and reality, uncertainty and stance, aloneness and coupling.

Reader comments

Carlene Tejada wrote:
Harrison Solow's approach to "Desire" mystifies me. Most of her critique centered on a word that did not appear in Alice's poem (betwixt). Had Solow perhaps seen an earlier version of the poem? I agree with her suggestions about removing italics from the word "his" and finding another way to mention values.

The final stanza of the poem struck me as being especially touching, metaphorical and ambiguous, thus open to a myriad of satisfying interpretations.

Alice Shapiro

Rae Spencer wrote:
I absolutely love the second stanza of this poem. For me, the first and third stanzas suffer by comparison, containing weaker metaphors and images. Also, the opening quotations overwhelm the poem, especially the second selection. I would be tempted to trim off the second quote (or both) and consider taking the first and third stanzas for use in a different poem. This would let the second stanza shine as a powerful individual poem.

Saltian

A son's war

Soldier, soldier
with angel cheeks of rosy hue
from the hike in sweltering heat
in mud and climbing hill upon hill
from the strike to an enemy
who stares back shocked
at a bullet's source
wishing then he could surrender
to prison instead of death.

Fresh and dewy,
a babe with gun
barely loosed from parents' grasp,
protects a country.
It is a concept large and altering
that builds strong leaders
where childhood once began.

Critique
By Kenneth Karrer

At its beginning the poem evokes Blake's "The Tyger." I've always loved that poem. Putting the two words "soldier" together side by side as it were could be something interesting to investigate at the poem's end or in the second verse. The early meter also evokes a sort of marching rhythm. There's a starkness in the first stanza which I find to be the poem's strength. That could be amplified by excising a word or two. I'd like to see the author consider dropping the words "sweltering" in line 3 and "climbing" in line 4 so that the poem would read:

Alice Shapiro

Soldier, soldier
with angel cheeks of rosy hue
from the hike
in heat,
in mud,
and hill upon hill.
From the strike
an enemy stares back
shocked
at a bullet's source
wishing then he could surrender
to a prison
instead of
death.

I also like the slight vagueness of the pronoun "he." The first thought is that it refers to the target of the bullet, but that's not necessarily so. I recommend ending the poem right there. The second stanza is not as mature as the first and distracts from the strength and simplicity of the first. A second verse could move to the commonalities of the two soldiers joined by death though that wouldn't necessarily require a stanza, maybe a line or two. This poem has great promise. Its writer hit a great vein.

Reader comments

Stan wrote:
Though I admire Blake's "The Tyger," I hear nothing of Blake's complexity in the poem. For me it sounds more nursery rhyme

like, which fights against the soberness of the message. Phrases like "cheeks of rosy hue" and "babe with gun" seem cliched, and I don't find much original in the poem, or at least it's 40 or 50 years behind the time when this sentiment was in vogue. I do agree with Kenneth that shorter is better.

Joanna wrote:
I do agree with Kenneth that that first verse is stronger than the second and works well solo. For the most part, I like his edits as well. I like that the poem's rhythm can be construed as either a marching rhythm OR a nursery rhyme—the side-by-side dichotomy of the two seems precisely to me to be what this piece is all about.

Alice Shapiro

Not my war

My first soldier was Dad.
The second I married.
In between I'd see a few
        here and there in supermarkets
        and on TV
but mostly passing by
as I offered hasty thank-you's
and after two broad, proud smiles
I to my kitchen
he to the fire.

Dad died from alcohol.
Joe's brain got cancer.
I'll never know his outcome
or if my words mattered.

Critique
By Kay Middleton

This excellent poem takes on several life truths. I am reminded that we marry our fathers for one reason or another. Then how we try to make a difference in their lives, at least we hope to. I liked the brevity of the poem and the fact that I wondered why the author "never knew his outcome ... " I always like it when a poem makes me wonder.

On the second read I was struck with the ownership of the soldiers, "My first ... the second ... " emphasized by the ones between that were seen but not numbered. The line "He to the fire" had several meanings for me: (1) The hearth/home; (2) gunfire; or (3) some substance or passion that is unnamed. Very effective.

I would suggest two changes. Line 1: "My first soldier was my father"—I prefer this because is sets a formal tone for the poem that is respectful and it creates an internal rhyme. Also, in the final lines the poet names the second soldier (Joe) so it is nice to call father "Dad" there, making the poem suddenly more personal. Line 5: spell out the word television. Again this makes the poem more formal and it balances the line lengths and I think improves the rhythm.

Finally, thanks to Alice Shapiro for the opportunity to comment on this very good work.

Reader comments

Jean wrote:
I enjoyed this poem very much and heartily agree with Ms. Middleton's balanced critique and suggestions.

Sarah wrote:
I too enjoyed this brief and affecting poem and Kay Middleton's insightful critique. I think the two suggested revisions (to Line 1 and Line 5) are excellent suggestions.

Alice Shapiro

Corporate war zones

One desk quiet
an open book cradled between two
fatted, idle hands;
one desk pressured to fulfill
dull tasks
at high speeds, perfectly
executed.

Un-
even
justice

Four white walls
with no ventilation
choking down indignation.
A war begins—
the bayonet of hate squashing hope
the guillotine, the trap
pushing back sparks of freedom.

"If a standard
blueprint rules
don't digress."

The crowd's most popular voice will drown the flower
less power to imitate the mating salmon
besieged in home-bound waters.

Yet, fame was still accomplished
by worthy ones

like V.P. Wallace Stevens, Einstein patent king
some unnamed, yet-to-be-discovered scholar
and one wonders
if the temperament of one's suffering
makes better art?

Critique
By David B Axelrod

I like a poem confident in its direction—one that uses fresh language, makes leaps and inventions with imagery, but also gives me confidence that I get it. I don't believe every poem must have a clear meaning. I certainly don't think there is only one interpretation for a poem. But with this poem, I read it several times and felt it did have a very specific intention/message. Thus, I revised it to quicken, unify, and clarify it.

Structurally, I went for consistent punctuation (which it mostly already had); a more regular line length (if not a regular measure); making each stanza have the same 10 lines.

I also took out abstractions that came too early to be earned by the opening stanzas. I got rid of the hyperbole of "bayonet ... guillotine ... freedom." None of that is needed. I think the poem now flows nicely to an important point. Nice work, Alice!

Corporate war zones

One desk is quiet,
an open book
cradled between two

Alice Shapiro

fatted, idle hands.
Another desk,
pressured to fulfill
dull tasks
at high speeds,
perfectly
executed.

Four white walls
with no ventilation
choking down indignation.
The crowd's voice
can drown the swimmer.　　　*Notice the change, so as not to*
　　　　　　　　　　　　　　　mix a metaphor below.

"Standard blueprint
rules. Don't digress."
Less power for the
salmon besieged in
home-bound waters.

Yet, fame is there
for the worthy ones
like V.P. Wallace Stevens,
Einstein the patent king,
or some unnamed, yet-
to-be-discovered scholar.
Still, one wonders
if such suffering
makes better art?

Saltian

Street wars

An illegal stole the identity
of one she thought dead
enlisted in the armed forces
saved her comrade's life
gave away a hero's medal
so as not to share her former misdeed
with a lurking INS.

He felt uneasy
but stuffed it down.

Turned around from natural law
exemplified by his neighbors
he reached for wrong behavior
bought someone's id card
drank and drugged
was brought to justice.

When sentenced for infractions
a sudden terror rose.
Confusion and unanswered questions
slid down his gut
until a displaced anger chose the gun
that fired at a harmless crowd.

Unaware,
she had set him up.

He idolized and followed
what transpired in the course of childhood.

Alice Shapiro

Armed with righteous indignation
we spat at them,
but who decided it was best
to see or do nothing
before the taking of their criminal acts?

Critique
By Ray Brown

I enjoy poems that are lyrical—tell a story—with mystery, suspense, leave the reader yearning for the answer. It is all the better if the reader is surprised by the outcome—and the poem leaves some gaps for the reader to fill with their imagination along the way. For that reason I appreciated this piece.

My personal preference would be for this poem to have left less mystery—made me, as a reader, work less to decipher the story. I will be interested in reading the reaction of others to this point, whether they find the uncertainties appeal to them more than the story.

Ms. Shapiro is a talented and skilled poet and each poet has their own writing style. I feel it is important for new writers to understand that there are alternate ways of expressing the same concepts so they can create their own deliberate style. I might have written the first stanza:

Saltian

She stole the identity
of one thought dead.
Enlisted in the armed forces
saved a comrade's life
declined a hero's medal
so as not to share her deeds
with a lurking INS.

Reader comments

Joanna wrote:
I agree with Ray here in that I enjoyed the lyrical, story-like feel of this piece. I also feel the plot just a tad muddy; to be honest I am still a little confused about who "she" and "he" are as characters and what they represent. I do find that opening stanza one of the strongest in the poem, and I like Ray's re-write equally well. The symmetry in the overall structure of the piece also works quite nicely given its back-and-forth flow.

Alice Shapiro

After war

Not a fan of war
I abhor violence in all its peculiarities
yet the warrior who fights injustice
knows the core of evil unbounded.

A bully must be beat
in a language understood
or thwarted like Mahatma did
wielding pacifistic love.

Where are the saints, the solvers?

In the ranks, trenches, holes
battling one on one
the horror
then coming home to concrete sorrow
wondering for the children destined
to cause the morbid death of flesh again.

Poised in a corner, covering his knees
blazing eyes turn terrified
the enemy within his head
nests and festers.

Under a crumbling wall
cold, a hand extended for a dime
he sings, surrenders to the rain
remembering the heat of battle.

It is a shame.

Critique: Responsive writing
Before war
By Bryan Borland

These are the daughters and sons
of America in all their curiosities:
school clothes in bandit gunfights,
candy rings on trigger fingers,
playground resurrections unlimited
and without repercussion.

The bully here is time. The bullies
are the geographies of our births.
They say no draft exists
but what of the socioeconomic lottery
of Small Town, Michigan,
where the factories have closed
and the only ways out
are blood oaths and mamas' tears?

Before war, a family of five
sits at a dinner table in Ohio.
They memorize the names
of villages in Afghanistan.
They learn the technology of absence;
the patriotism of the missing.

The oldest will leave in two days
and when he returns, the Medusa
of conflict will have changed his upturned palms

to stone. One day, those palms
will face our direction. Stone ourselves,
we will pass in silence.

We will be ashamed.

Responsive Photo
By Bryan Borland

Reader comments

omar wrote:
Phenomenal posts! I love the call and response and the open-ended, high-quality expressiveness and beauty.

Saltian

Distant wars

> *You cannot simultaneously prevent*
> *and prepare for war.*
> —Albert Einstein

Brush-hidden jungle shrieks
fly at soldiers' eyes.
Bat-like, they swoop to target.
Unawares, the heart-beat
races
alert.
Safe.
When rivals yield and reconcile
carrion in dreams still appear.
In time break-downs lapse
as memory's duty dwindles
blessedly in the art of love.

Sons and daughters trade their freedom
for us.

Encrypted screens
in digital form
blast off legs, arms.
Distanced by machines
safe,
no harm juxtaposed
by giving killing signals,
the game remains
a general's numbing verbal order.

Sons and daughters learn a trade.

Alice Shapiro

Critique
By Charles Clifford Brooks III

This is a noble first run at not only what "war" has been to the human race, but what it is becoming. I see the evolution of battle in the mention of the new "digital age" of struggle that I remember first seeing in the CNN coverage of Desert Storm. It seemed on that eerie, green screen that the deaths of so many were reduced to a video game. This poem does a good job of marrying the present/future with the age-old dark side of human nature.

Yet, the language here could benefit from being taken out of a general sense. Poetry shouldn't be needlessly cryptic (which this isn't), but some room for wonder isn't a bad thing. The oldest rule of poetry I can remember is, "Show, don't tell." There is an abundant amount of telling here with a sliver of show. There is obviously a clear connection mentally and emotionally between the poet and this topic. A suggestion is to add a viewpoint that knocks at the back door or climbs through a window.

There is no room to argue that the blood poured into this piece is from a deep, deep place (almost) beyond words. The main suggestion I have is to put a fresh eye on the language and rediscover a way to retell the tale from an unexpected angle. This is an exciting start where war is fleshed out to remind us all that pain comes before, during, and well after the first shot.

Saltian

Worst wars

A cancerous child desired to be a soldier.
Granted this, he spent a day and night
in bivouacs, rifle drills, exercising
in and out of rubber tires
scaling walls with a gentle lift
from combat buddies.
His lit-up face among the giants
towering over his frailty
was prize enough for those who organized
his brief and poignant tour of duty.

Most young boys imagining a toy war
go home to dinner
with all four limbs, bullet-free abdomens
and scar-less psyches
unlike a soldier's life
that is envied unaware of consequences.

And thanks abound
for a youngster's dream-world
grown to fight
disarm an enemy
protect us
from a threatened harm.
And so a country's choices must
bear delicate scrutiny
while sending idealistic soldier-boys
and girls
off to die.

Alice Shapiro

The child whose illness
brought him early access
to a war zone
in the fore-days of his death
died happy, free
of more than one reality.

Critique
By KC Bosch

This well-written, cleverly worded poem is my favorite Alice Shapiro piece. The telling paints a picture of everyone involved except the country making the decisions, making choices that will put their idealistic young children in harm's way. The ending, both happy and sad, is very striking. Thank you for writing this and letting me comment.

My only issue (other than ones regarding the politics of war) is with the third stanza, which feels disjointed. After several readings it still does not flow for me.

Saltian

Laze away the day

Love morning
late and lazy
love that

cat curling
up bottom of the bed
not time yet

sun washes
over sheets and pillows
approaching moon

June Summers
perplex the dead-
hearted naysayers.

Bedding none
of their dreams
they run to work again.

Critique
By Ashok Karra

It's a fun poem to read and reread: you've done a great job with the sounds, letting those "L"s linger in the first stanza and allowing those very suggestive "sh" sounds in the third stanza to speak. What exactly does the speaker of the poem want us to shush about?

Alice Shapiro

There seems to be a hidden contention. Is the comfort we take lazing around in bed the same thing as sensuality? A first consideration of the problem yields an emphatic "no." Last I checked, it's a lot of work to go to the club or bar, chat, drink and dance, and hopefully get digits. Nowadays people pay thousands for weekend courses in order to improve their "game" or whatever the kids call it. But your poem's speaker builds the contention slowly. "Late and lazy" implies strongly there is no "morning" for us if we are at work right away. "Love that" doesn't just flow into the cat's behavior of the second stanza, but leaves whatever "morning" is open. The cat curls; the circular motion takes us away from linear orderings ("up bottom") and thus away from time. This has to be sensual bliss; the sun isn't a neutral observer but actively washing, suggesting prelapsarian innocence. The poem does a terrific job of hiding that, and we have to wonder whether the pride we take in getting digits is another sort of game. Truly erotic desires may lack the ambition of a chase. Maybe what marks most desires is that they can actually be fulfilled.

The sun introduces time to the poem ("noon," "June," "Summers") and the speaker is attentive to the progression. Time is literally looming larger for speaker, audience, and anyone spoken about —those returning to work. If you want to amend this poem, I'd probably enlarge its scope a bit: how are the naysayers perplexed? The sun merely scorches them, and they retreat into air conditioning. "Again" suggests they have the circular motion of the cat, and that brings forth another consideration. The speaker moves seamlessly from "late and lazy" to "dreams." Even

Saltian

though I've talked above about how erotic longings could be ambitionless, this is not a point without some controversy. My own reading of Xenophon makes this emphatic—can the tyrant be defined as one whose erotic longings are so great he must rule no matter what? "Dreams" take us away from lazing around and may even take us away from sensual bliss. This is perhaps a point connected with my reading of poetry generally. I'm not sold on omniscient narrators. I'd rather hear a voice that articulates something and in articulation runs up against a limit. Usually that happens ironically without the speaker's knowledge, eg, Yeats' "Sailing to Byzantium." One could say, though, the speaker hid the contention because thinking through it would deny the "laziness" so romantically described. So I don't know. I just know I enjoyed reading the poem.

Reader comments

ashok wrote:
If you're interested in a poem with a similar setup—just lying around in bed—see Jane Kenyon's "Dark Morning: Snow."
http://www.ashokkarra.com/2011/06/jane-kenyon-dark-morning-snow/

Jean wrote:
I loved the dreamy drowse of the poem, taking a cue, perhaps incorrectly, from the fact that it represented the section, Dementia and Death, of *Saltian*, that the narrator mused on earlier times as s/he lay in bed while sunlight turned to moon and awaited death. Yes, oft-times, I really AM just this concrete.

Alice Shapiro

Annmarie wrote:
Oops! A typo! The last word of line 9 should be "noon" instead of "moon." So sorry! But here's the cool part: Ashok Karra's commentary refers to "noon" in reference to the importance of the concept of time to the poem, and Jean's comment refers to the passage of time as "sunlight turned to the moon." So I ask you, dear readers, which word do you prefer here: noon or moon?

Stan wrote:
Though I often write very literally, I think "moon" actually offers a stronger image, even if it isn't meant literally. How a sun turns to moon is much more ambiguous than the sun turning to noon.

Lawrence Berger wrote:
Alice, In the poems I've looked at you do a great job of describing what you see. but what about the other four senses? What do you hear, smell, taste or touch? A "list poem" is fine every once in a while, but if that's all you offering I don't think I'd buy the book. Neither will most people.

ashok wrote:
@Lawrence Berger—Alice has done a terrific job working through what for Plato and Aristotle was the chief sense. "Sight" connects human being with rationality, the distance between man and object our mind has to bridge in its finitude. That was enough of a theme for Sophocles to work with in *Oedipus Rex*. Oedipus never really understands man standing upright, with the full scope of his vision. Of the Sphinx's riddle, Oedipus literally corresponds with the old man (Oedipus' swollen feet means he probably walks with a cane) and the infant.

Saltian

I could go on, but you're not worth talking to. The only reason I wrote this is that Alice deserves a defense and deserves an audience.

Rae Spencer wrote:
This poem is a fun, soft recollection. Unlike Lawrence Berger, I think the poem is rich in touch and sound: the warm cat and sunlight, the rumpled sheets and pillows, and the near silence of a room given over to sleep. I admire that the poem does not attempt to sketch the scene further. It gives me a few details to start from, then lets my own memory take the wheel.

Alice Shapiro

The law of attraction

> *A man is like a cat, chase him and*
> *he will run—sit still and ignore him*
> *and he'll come purring at your feet.*
> —Helen Rowland, English-American writer (1896-1950)

This is the Abstract:
Within reach
the prize hovers
yet still she hides a former lack
as someone else's fare.

Almost there,
she wonders where the change began
between the stress of *"get it," "get it"*
and the seamless streaming flow.

She was knighted without her knowledge
without attention or control.
It is hard to let go
easy to slip, like a drunkard denying drink

back to active force through effort.
She knows that batter must be stirred
by human hands
but only fire bakes sweet cakes.

This is the tale:
A man of former wealth, now vagabond
who suffered sudden lapses into dark mind
once taught a girl a lesson
more kind than cash.

Saltian

He commanded her to stillness
while first he cursed
the wife who sealed
his present prison fate.

Continuing, he berated mother
for committing him to hell
upon his former spouse's
unjust recommendation.

The curious crowd noticed from nearby
as if they were swayed by a Syrian flute
that wakes a sleeping snake
and glued their eyes to his dramatic, irate state.

He rambled. She listened.

The rock of sheer solid steady sitting
caused awe and interest
did not betray the fact that here
there was mostly nothing.

She saw how attitude begets impressions
and slowed-down actions
bring attention away from "there"
towards "here."

This is the outcome:
Equal in mental disfiguration
they gained a bond.
Years passed.

Alice Shapiro

An intruding link from that distance
recalled the wisdom she now needed
that a sad and fractured millionaire once imparted.

He mentored her
and proved that when in need
she should emulate the loss of tension

which activates the future
blessed, unharmed, lucrative,
charmed.

Critique
By Hans Ostrom

Yes, learning to do nothing is something special, as is unlearning. To obey the laws of attraction, one must sometimes disobey the instincts of attraction, and in writing a narrative poem, one must resist the urge to tell a story. Paradox is the perfect logic of poetry, which is attracted to contradiction and likes to break laws peacefully. Poetry has its detractors, who don't know what they're missing and miss what they don't know. In poetry, *there* becomes *here*.

Reader comments

Joanna wrote:
I like the way the section breaks are full sentences here. Not sure why exactly, but they really work for me. And that last verse in "Abstract" about the batter and the cake really made my mind pop. Brilliant. Having said that, I have to confess I like Hans Ostrom's critique almost as much as I like the piece—it's poetry in and of itself.

Saltian

On walls

Onto the far wall
I create imaginary
fanciful décor
to satisfy my
perfection compulsion
to order everything
to place objects
in spaces whose effects
may please the eye.

Walls so covered do not breathe.
"Leave them bare" I threaten
and when the impulse
beckons like a drug
I should let go and find the beauty
elsewhere
like in the imperfections
of dried paint, bubbled
solidified as white embossed
on white.

The Abstract Expressionists
must have seen this
as they swept away the past
completely
leaving scratches, undefined
explosions of shape, color,
non-confirming minutiae adorning
the nature of paint on walls.
Yet, content with status
no wall of habit ends.

Alice Shapiro

Critique
By Bill Yarrow

Interesting poem in which the idea of decoration has analogies with the process of writing itself. This could, however, be made more explicit in the poem. There is potential for the narrative "I" to undergo more of a transformation than is evident here.

Suggestions:
- Capitalize "walls" in the title
- Have all stanzas have the same number of lines: currently 9, 10, 10.
- "On the far wall"—of what? Create a specific location for the poem.
- "imaginary/fanciful décor"—I'd rather "see" the décor than be have it be described generally—specifics would work well here.
- Delete "perfection"—"to satisfy my/compulsion/to order everything" reads better.
- "to place objects/in spaces whose effects/may please the eye"—as a reader, I'd like to know more specifically what those intended "effects" are. Consider an unexpected, specific adjective in front of "effects."
- "Walls so covered do not breathe"—this seems to be an inner voice to counter the "I" in the first stanza, but, again, as a reader, I would like to know what "so covered" means. I'd like to have that refer to something visual and specific.
- "Leave them bare" is the "I" responding. Rather than have the "I" in italics, I think the inner voice should be in italics. I prefer
    Walls so covered do not breathe.
    "Leave them bare," I threaten.

- "and when the impulse/beckons like a drug"—"beckons" is too mild a word to be associated with the addictive pull of a drug.
- "and when the impulse/beckons like a drug/I should let go and find the beauty/elsewhere"—the logic is confused here. There's a piece of the argument missing. The idea seems to be "When the impulse to cover the walls asserts itself, I should resist the impulse and instead look for beauty elsewhere."
- "find the beauty/elsewhere"—the use of the phrase "the beauty" here feels too abstract. Tweak the phrase perhaps to soften and enliven it.
- "like in the imperfections/of dried paint, bubbled/solidified as white embossed/on white"—the specifics here are very good. Delete "like"—it's unnecessary. Delete "the" also.
- If this were me, I'd go for one precise image: "in imperfections/of dried/white paint"; "bubbled," "solidified" and "embossed" are all implied in "imperfections" of paint.
- "The Abstract Expressionists/must have seen this"—very good. Echo of Auden in "Musee des Beaux Arts."
- "as they swept away the past"—I'm not sure the Abstract Expressionists really did sweep away the past. That's an arguable point. Can you insert an adjective before "past" to make the phrase more pointed, more argumentative, more memorable?
- Delete "completely"—it doesn't add anything. Let "Swept away" do its work.
- "leaving scratches, undefined/explosions of shape, color,"—good. I particularly like the use of "explosions." Is there a better alternative to "undefined"? "Amorphous" perhaps?

Alice Shapiro

- "non-confirming minutiae"—not sure what "non-confirming" refers to. Typo for "non-conforming"? Confused by the phrase. "Minutiae" is too abstract—I'd like a specific detail in its place. Give an example, perhaps, of the Abstract Expressionist style.
- "adorning" is too precious a word here—find a replacement.
- "adorning/the nature of paint on walls."—the logic here is tangled. Surely the "explosions of shape, color" "adorn" the walls themselves, not "the nature of paint on walls." If another idea is meant, it is not expressed clearly enough for the reader, and the clause should be revised.
- "Yet, content with status"—good phrase, but perhaps expand or explain this "status." Is "status quo" meant? Comma is unnecessary and should be deleted. It blocks the line and the connection between "yet" and "content."
- "no wall of habit ends"—that's an interesting ending phrase and idea: "wall of habit" is not immediately decipherable but is resonant in the poem, bringing the reader back to stanza one. I'd like the idea, however, to be clarified or expanded on. What is really happening at the end of this poem? Is the "I" going back to the compulsion of decorating with "pleasing effects"? If so, the speaker has learned nothing in the second and third stanzas. Shouldn't there be some sort of transformation effected here? I'd like to see the lessons of the Abstract Expressionists be exhibited in this poem. Similarly, the qualities of Abstract Expressionism could be worked more specifically into the language choices in this poem.

Saltian

Rich man, poor man

Wise owls hoot and saw fine proverbs
wise-asses crow loud as a neighbor's chanticleer
or speak sly like Pharisees before the cleansing.

The satiated merchant
rests upon his brocade chair
goaded on by hangers-on.
Having gathered wealth and fame
he crosses arms above his bloated gut
not knowing if his friend is present
for a tat advice and fine chatter
or duty for a share of this man's money cache.

As if from a deep black hole
alone, he looks back wondering:
Given this poor end
would a different path
have provided satisfaction,
a wife and children
instead of boundless circles
of sycophants?

Too late. It is done, this career.
He awaits another stage to appear
to teach elusive, unachievable perfection.

Alice Shapiro

Critique
By Carlene Tejada

This poem increases my respect for Alice Shapiro's word choice. She doesn't need long and wordy descriptions. In the 1st stanza, "sly" gives the image of officials whispering behind columns. In the 2nd stanza, "brocade" suggests the decorative environment of the wealthy. In the 3rd stanza, "circles of sycophants" suggest a medieval court filled with needy, easily disloyal subjects. The imagery is further enhanced by the repetition of long and strong vowel sounds and initial and internal consonance. I am uncomfortable with the first two lines because nature and the barnyard do not fit the exotic tone of the following line and stanzas. The word "tat" refers to a specific kind of needlework and seems out of place here.

Like Alice's other poems, this one trembles with ambiguity. Does "another stage ... unachievable perfection" refer to an afterlife or to the merchant's hope that it's not "Too late" and another stage could bring him closer to perfection? I'm reminded of wealthy, aging Buddhists who give away their riches and wander the countryside holding a begging bowl. Is that what awaits the merchant? Is this when he expects to be taught "unachievable perfection" or must he wait for lessons in Heaven or Hell? Certainly, by our contemporary standards, perfection won't be found in Shakespeare's "last scene of all ... Sans teeth, sans eyes, sans taste, sans everything."

What price has the merchant/justice paid for wisdom, fame and wealth? Is it true wisdom if in the latter stages of life he lacks progeny and true friends? He has lived selfishly and still thinks only of himself as he faces the next phase.

Denial

When one has done most everything
that a childish mind desires—

white-haired and haberdashered
the thread about to unravel
the chink in the champagne glass
about to lengthen
subordinates' sneers increasing,
attrition in its infancy
is quietly noticed

and pushed down like so much salt
at ocean's bottom.

Critique: Responsive Writing
Realization
By Maxwell Baumbach

I can't stand to look at me now

my parents installed an escalator
along the side of my favorite mountain
so that I could reach the heights I dreamed of
yet
still
amazingly
I was too lazy to climb

I never chased anything—
I followed with a brisk mosey at best

Alice Shapiro

the escalator no longer functions
it's just a set of stairs now
and I have to put in the work to get at the top
but it's too late
I don't have it in me anymore to do so
and the reality is I never did
but it had been pushed down like so much salt
at ocean's bottom that I could do whatever I pleased

Saltian

Where is the justice in that?

Young minds think mature
despite a jumbled slew of words
spitted out.
Agape at the wisdom of babes
one wonders is it fair
that word cells die
leaving spaces where once lied places
of good times spent,
names and faces now rent of links
to anything?

At the rise of an insult
that child's brash brain formed responses
strong enough to drain the blood
of her attacker
but lacked a physical skill
to mouth explicit answers.
In these far days it is common
to hear her loud and gritty verbal grumbles
near every visitor's exit, every tumble
with a neighbor.

Critique
By John Gosslee

The concept of Shapiro's book is interesting and the poem "Where is the justice in that?" must build from the other works in the manuscript. It is difficult to understand what it is about as a singular poem.

Alice Shapiro

The first sentence makes an unqualified statement that goes unexplained throughout the poem. How many readers will read "... agape" as "mouth wide open" or as the greek love term?

Word cells, good time spent, physical skill, explicit answers, and verbal grumbles are elusive descriptors that would work best as concrete images. A comma after line 4 in stanza 2 is recommended and the poem needs some overall grammar improvements. I am looking forward to seeing the next draft.

Reader comments

Ray Sharp wrote:
I think "spat out" is the common preterite and past participle form; not spitted, but I could be wrong. Two forms are often accepted. Also, should "once lay" be the past tense of "to lie"?

Joanna wrote:
I also feel a little unclear about Shapiro's meaning here. Is she protesting the overuse of verbal retaliation to insult? Lamenting the loss of the ability to create language as one ages? I also agree with John that a comma would help after line 4 in cuing the reader in to the start of the next thought. Ray, you're the grammar expert; do you think "spit out" might be another alternative in the opening lines, to keep with the present tense "think" in that same phrase? I agree that "lied" should be "lay," although I appreciate that the internal rhyme ("die/lied"; "spent/rent") is somewhat lost by this replacement. I love the image conjured by "word cells"!

Saltian

Well done

I. Presently

I—peruse past decades
I—have accomplished greatness
I—overcame

arcane banality
self-doubt
impetuous naivete

Tender errors at ten and twenty
baked into inner walls of an open mind
formed a calloused heart.

II. Looking back

Barefoot
walking sand-drenched sidewalks in the tropics
dazed, yet unfazed by a temporary lapse
in continuity

God—at my back

arcane banality—self-doubt
      went up like smoke.

III. Future

Purified
wise wide innocence shares my easy chair
I—consider grace.

Alice Shapiro

Critique
By Walter Elmore

I. Presently
I—peruse past decades
I—have accomplished greatness
I—overcame
x arcane banality
x self-doubt
x impetuous naiveté
Tender errors at ten and twenty
baked onto inner walls of an open mind
formed a calloused heart.
II. Looking back
Barefoot
walking sand-drenched sidewalks in the tropics
dazed, yet unfazed by a temporary lapse
in continuity
God—at my back
x arcane banality—self-doubt
went up like smoke.
III. Future
Purified
wise wide innocence shares my easy chair
I—consider grace.

The structure presents itself like a to-do list but has the content of a memoir. Interestingly, "errors at ten and twenty" are placed in the "Presently" section, even though they bring to mind ages and years past. As well, the conflict between "open mind" and "calloused heart" paints an interesting yet very human picture of a person who struggles to see past the end of his or her nose without being too gullible or easily persuaded. Another interesting dualism is the use of the adjective "wise" to modify the noun "innocence." One normally doesn't equate wisdom with innocence, although small children are known for spots of brilliance too often dismissed because of their age. The points at which "arcane banality" and "self-doubt" appear in both the present and past lists remind me of how we put these things behind us, even though they continue to crop up time and again.

Alice Shapiro

Original face

> *If I had only known,*
> *I would have been a locksmith.*
> —Albert Einstein

The man
white, gut-flab, white flakes
scattered on a navy-jacket shoulder
walks the foyer, sweeps over
marble squares in flip-toed satin slippers.

The man drops his heavy frame—
mutton-stuffed, driven here and there—
upon a velvet cushion. Sighs.
His woes encumber, restrict all movement.

Still and glassy eyes flicker at each grumble:

—the note that's due
—the errant worker
—the crumbling empire

How long it stood, a fine Fort Knox
building gold, prospering empty pockets.

As the crimson embers fade
and a gray chill begets a hemorrhage
of reckoning
he sees, in one gloss
the dream before the dream.

Saltian

Critique
By David B Axelrod

Original face

> *If I had only known,*
> *I would have been a locksmith.*
> —Albert Einstein

The man	*Why mention that he is white? perhaps, instead, he is pale?*
white, gut-flab, white flakes	*"gut" is jarring, more so hyphenated. Why not "flabby?"*
scattered on a navy-jacket shoulder	*Dandruff is disconcerting enough. Leave out the navy color.*
walks the foyer, sweeps over marble squares in flip-toed satin slippers.	*I can't picture "flip-toed."*
The man drops his heavy frame— mutton-stuffed, driven here and there— upon a velvet cushion. Sighs.	*He's a lamb eater? Cushion? Is it on the floor? "Couch?"*
His woes encumber, restrict all movement.	*"restrict?" He's walking?*
Still and glassy eyes flicker at each grumble:	*If they flicker, are they still?*

Alice Shapiro

—the note that's due
—the errant worker
—the crumbling empire

How long it stood, a fine Fort Knox
building gold, prospering empty pockets.   *Nice lines to characterize a business...*

As the crimson embers fade   *Is there a fireplace nearby or a metaphor for failure?*
and a gray chill begets a hemorrhage   *"hemorrhage" does go with "crimson."*
of reckoning
he sees, in one gloss   *Interesting use of "gloss."*

the dream before the dream.   *This ties in with Einstein and our lacking foresight.*

Thus I would rewrite this:

Original face

*If I had only known,
I would have been a locksmith.*

—Albert Einstein

Saltian

The man, pale,
flabby, white flakes
scattered on his shoulders,
walks the foyer, sweeps over
marble squares in satin slippers.

He drops his heavy frame
on a velvet couch. Sighs, his woes
encumbering his movement.
His dark-ringed eyes flicker at each grumble:

—the note that's due
—the errant worker
—the crumbling empire

How long it stood, a fine Fort Knox,
building gold, prospering empty pockets.

As its crimson embers fade,
a gray chill begets a hemorrhage
of reckoning,
he sees, in one gloss,
the dream before the dream.

This is a fine poem, given our current economy with all its
sordid revelations, ruined careers and enterprises that we have
witnessed. It encapsulates both the man and the greater vanity of
human wishes.

Alice Shapiro

Injustice

I might assume you mean to say
I am lovely and dear
and once I would have been assured
of this.

Now you stare, blank and faraway
more salient thoughts beckon your attention.

I could ramble endlessly
about fantastic things
and you would simply nod
agreeably.

Open those eyes and look, look again!
I am here and waiting for your refrain.

Sing it, speak it low and indistinct
but gather muster just this once
allow my dried, outdated illusions
like a fashion faux pas not yet new and chic.

You give me pause.
I am not fond of this injustice.

Critique
By Julie Ellinger Hunt

At first read, this concise poem illustrates simple yet enjoyable poetic elements such as style and theme. I initially considered it to be simplistic overall, but as I went back and read it through again, the poem opened up like soft petals on a flower, revealing something quite special.

There is solace and grace, as the narrator walks us through the reality of being with one another after a bit of time. That newness is gone. That excitement. That thrill. She is standing firm and saying, "Look, I am still here!" as his attention focuses on things more exhilarating. I feel like this is so relatable and real. Anyone who has been in a marriage or long relationship can understand this raw emotion and want to smack him in the head and say, "Yo, Dumbass! Look at her!"

Responsive Art
Salient Love
By Julie Ellinger Hunt

Alice Shapiro

Stan wrote:
Yes, Julie is right in that the poem seems simple but carries a great weight (gracefully). The tone is one of wearied patience which so many of us can identify with, even if it hasn't been very long in a relationship. I have 2 thoughts to add. The first really has nothing to do with the revising the poem, and that is "I wonder what she did to shut him down—and whatever it was, she doesn't have a clue." That's probably just a male response, knowing that there are two sides to an issue. The second, unfortunately, is the last 2 lines. They feel like they shift from the "show" mode to the "tell mode." The poem would be even stronger if those lines could be pulled from the reader without having to state it. The title tips the reader that way. Consider if there are descriptive lines that could replace them, or if the poem might really end at "chic."

And Julie's picture is fabulous; the tipped heart and the face-propped woman capture the mood of the poem so so well.

Maxwell Baumbach wrote:
First off, the poem is absolutely beautiful. "I could ramble endlessly/about fantastic things/and you would simply nod/agreeably." That stanza perfectly illustrates what you were getting at. It's one of those stanzas where you look at it, and there is nothing to be changed. Simply beautiful.

Secondly, the art done by Julie is equally astonishing. Grabbing, telling, and fitting for the piece you were to respond to.

Good job to both of you.

Saltian

Sarah wrote:
I agree that this stanza in particular is really spot on.

Scott Owens wrote:
So what are her "dried, outdated illusions"? A belief in enduring romantic love? A self-concept of undying beauty and allure? The previous poem contained a nice seemingly contradictory juxtaposition ("depth of ascension") that could be easily understood to suggest how we get wrapped up or lost in ambition. This poem has a similar contradictory juxtaposition ("outdated" and "not yet new"). Unlike the first one, this just doesn't work all that well for me. I suppose it depends upon the trend in fashion for the old to become new again, but by the time I ferret all of that out of the words, I'm no longer interested. On another note, to quibble a bit with Stan, I think love often ends without either partner bearing the responsibility. I don't think she would necessarily have to have done anything "to shut him down." In a poem of my own called "The End of Love," I use the phrase "the inexplicable growth of unfulfillment."

Stan wrote:
Not a quibble, I hope, so much as an alternative. I don't need to cast blame on either party. The poem does, though, point out the male's inattention that is hurting the female. It goes the other way as well, just not in this poem. I'd be happy to see your poem, as well.

Alice Shapiro

Scott Owens wrote:
My quibble was to your suggestion that the speaker had necessarily done something "to shut him down." I agree that either party can lose interest, but often it happens without intention. In other words, without anyone consciously "doing" anything. My poem is due out from *Referential Magazine* in the near future, so instead of posting it here, I'll email it to you.

Saltian

Sand and photographs

His grown son's photographs rested in my view.
His name in sand appeared,
caused a thought, and it was seized
fast without considering, without propriety.
I looked and looked and stared.

Once it was told he carried
the face of his father.
I peered hard at the page
gazing at the possibility
that I might catch his carbon copy countenance
to hold it in my heart again
renew an old and distant feeling
but what peered back was silence.
This was not my child, nor my soul.
He was hers.

It did not matter
as I peered further
into the eyes of his son's son
again with wonder and expectation
extinguished.

Almost gone, like his smile upon my entrance,
the scratches in beach sand
spelling out his name
are frozen forever on film.
The ocean now can never wash away
every microscopic trace of him

Alice Shapiro

and one could look as often as one wanted
to see that name,
recapture loving
a taste of salt hinting at what could have been.

Critique
By Rae Spencer

In "Sand and photographs," the poet employs wonderful verb choices (ie, "rested," "seized," and "frozen") to establish a feeling of time suspended, a prolonged moment of introspection. The use of pronouns rather than names invites careful consideration for each mention of "his" and "he." When the speaker says, "He was hers," is this "he" the father or the son? Is she acknowledging a lost romance or lost possibility of family? By leaving these question unanswered, the author admirably illustrates the complexity of "what if…?"

In the last stanza, I found myself dwelling on the switch in perspective from the speaker's first person "I" to the more distant third person "one" ("…one could look as often as one wanted…"). Why not "…I could look as often as I wanted…"? Or why not echo the tense of "The ocean now can never…" with "…I can look as often as I want…"? For me, the subtle shift in focus disrupted my rapport with the speaker. However, the connection was quickly re-established with the instantly recognizable "taste of salt."

Taken line by line, there are places in every poem worthy of in-depth discussion. As an example, consider this line from the second stanza: "but what peered back was silence." At least one alternate phrasing is immediately obvious, "but silence peered back." I prefer the author's choice, because I like how the line fades in sound with the soft syllables of "silence." In a different poem, I might argue the opposite. What about other readers? Do they also prefer the author's choice? And what about the first line of that stanza? What alternatives are available for "Once it was told he carried," and how did the author decide?

I would like to thank Alice Shapiro and Annmarie Lockhart for inviting me to take part in this unique and fascinating process. I am in awe of Ms. Shapiro's courage.

Reader comments

Joanna wrote:
I agree with Rae that there is a wonderful sense of "what if ... " or, as Shapiro puts it, "what could have been ... " in this piece that demonstrates delicately the quiet, soul-tearing sensation of having universes slip through one's fingertips.

Rae highlights the line "but what peered back was silence" and offers an alternative phrase, "but silence peered back." I agree with her here again that Shapiro's original line is stronger. For me, though, it's not about the fading in the sound of "silence," but in the rhythm given to the line due to the greater number of syllables; somehow it follows more easily from the previous lines when worded this way.

Alice Shapiro

On a related note, I very much like the echo of "peered" ("I peered hard at the page ... but what peered back was silence.") in that verse, but would like to have heard another word (bored? focused?) in place of the repetition again of "peered" in the following verse ("as I peered further"). Alternately, Ms. Shapiro might even consider cutting the third stanza entirely, bringing the longer verses on either side of it into sharper focus.

One final point on which Rae and I are in complete agreement: Ms. Shapiro definitely has no shortage of courage.

Rae Spencer wrote:
I like Joanna's suggestion to cut the third stanza, and I'm intrigued by how that revision would affect the first stanza. Could it be cut, too, and therefore preserve symmetry in line count?

For me, the first stanza contains a few critical elements: the words "rested," "seized," and "stared." However, these verbs can be incorporated into the second stanza, successfully replacing verbs that are either repeated later in the poem or contribute less. For example: "I stared hard at the page/seized by the possibility/that his carbon copy countenance/might rest in my heart again."

As for the first stanza's contribution to setting and scene, the title already introduces both the sand and the photographs, though in this case it might benefit from being reversed: "Photographs and sand." (The first section of Chapter Three, in Ted Kooser's

Saltian

Poetry Home Repair Manual, changed the way I think about poem titles.)

The third stanza is less troublesome. Removing it requires no adjustment to the rest of the poem and, in my opinion, improves the poem's focus and narrative.

I'm interested in what Alice Shapiro makes of these suggestions. I have enjoyed following WIP: *Saltian*, but I had hoped for more response from the author.

Alice Shapiro

Not there yet

I hear of some who live eight decades
hear their bones creak like old oak staircases
see strained movements captured
in slow motion, like being bathed,
not royally in milk with Caesar's twelve attendants,
but wretched and pained.

My friend wails at forgotten faces he cannot place
as if erased and unborn.
Who can come to him at ninety
replace a broken body, restore dead cells
that once held bold humanity?

Fresh and supple children
uninitiated and anathema to their own Fate
deride and scold
laying him beneath their feet
even once he raised them up.

I hear his lament:
"Old age ain't no picnic."
Thus far, in the thick of project after project,
I barely hear the drummer
contemplate instead a full and fancy future.

Critique
By Courtney Leigh Jameson

It was very difficult to analyze the context of this poem since I have not yet read the Saltian monologue by Shakespeare. With that being said, my analysis of "Not there yet" may be only two dimensional, although I had to dive into this poem deeply to forge an understanding. I gathered that this poem is about a friend who may be dying from old age or a terminal illness and is observing the old and decrepit dying naturally, and the young and strong growing up to inevitably die as well.

There were several facets of this poem that made it extremely confusing (besides not having read the monologue), including the many subjects. The poem goes from "some who live eight decades" to "my friend wails" to "who can come to him" to "fresh and supple children" to "once he raised," and then a drummer is brought in at the end. Too many of these subjects in the poem raise a lot of questions as to who these people are, why are they important to the overall meaning of this poem, and by using all of these subjects what is at stake? It might be best to name the friend from the beginning and then refer to him later as a he. Another confusing aspect are the cliche lines. "Old oak staircase" would be better conveyed as the "old staircase," "wails" sounds too Beowulfish, and "fresh and supple children" is kind of disturbing and not in a good way because it does not convey their youth, but rather something more sensual about these children, and "bold humanity" should be extinguished because isn't humanity bold already by being strong enough to slowly die while remaining alive (being old, ultimately)? The last 3 lines confuse me at the end because I am not sure who the drummer is and exactly what it is he is contemplating. (When I think of the word "contemplating" in the subject of life or death, it makes me think the subject is contemplating suicide and I am not sure if that is what you were going for.)

Alice Shapiro

This poem was written very well and the language is sophisticated, but I think the images get lost easily. The first stanza has strong imagery and then it becomes more abstract as I read on. My suggestion would be to condense it, take some of the abstractions out (like "uninitiated and anathema to their own fate"), and focus more of the image/observation of the friend dying, rather than your observations of all of these outside influences.

Side note: If anyone else, like myself, read this poem without understanding the context, they might be just as confused. Be aware of your audience. I am not sure if I was the best person to read this particular poem because I did read it out of context and it was very hard for me to grasp the meaning or even what was going on. There are some mechanical issues which I had noted. The images are very strong, but there are not very many of them and they get confused with all of the abstract words/images. Thank you for this opportunity and I will understand if you decide not to use my critique.

Reader comments

Jean wrote:
Courtney, why not read Shakespeare's Seven Stages of Man before doing your critique? It's only two hundred twelve words:

All the world's a stage,
And all the men and women merely players;
They have their exits and their entrances,
And one man in his time plays many parts,
His acts being seven ages. At first, the infant,

Saltian

Mewling and puking in the nurse's arms.
Then the whining schoolboy, with his satchel
And shining morning face, creeping like snail
Unwillingly to school. And then the lover,
Sighing like furnace, with a woeful ballad
Made to his mistress' eyebrow. Then a soldier,
Full of strange oaths and bearded like the pard,
Jealous in honour, sudden and quick in quarrel,
Seeking the bubble reputation
Even in the canon's mouth. And then the justice,
In fair round belly with good capon lined,
With eyes severe and beard of formal cut,
Full of wise saws and modern instances;
And so he plays his part. The sixth age shifts
Into the lean and slippered pantaloon
With spectacles on nose and pouch on side;
His youthful hose, well saved, a world too wide
For his shrunk shank, and his big manly voice,
Turning again toward childish treble, pipes
And whistles in his sound. Last scene of all,
That ends this strange eventful history,
Is second childishness and mere oblivion,
Sans teeth, sans eyes, sans taste, sans everything.

Rae Spencer wrote:
I think Courtney Leigh Jameson is absolutely correct when she says, "If anyone else, like myself, read this poem without understanding the context, they might be just as confused."

Alice Shapiro

For me, this entire project raises a question about context. "Not there yet" is part of a collection. As such, is it necessary for the poem to stand as an individual creation, as a complete and separate work of art?

I am accustomed to reading poems as individual works published in journals. Rarely do I find more than five poems by any one author in a single issue. Even in those cases, the poems cannot rely on context for their meaning. I expect each poem to be a single, fully developed entity.

Should I have the same expectation for poems that are part of a poetry collection? Is it acceptable, perhaps even desirable, for poems within a collection to remain opaque as individual works and only reveal clarity when viewed in context?

Stan wrote:
There are two answers, of course. For me, a poem needs to stand alone. When it is gathered into the collection, then the synergy of the poems goes beyond the original strength of the individual poem. That said, there are some (weaker?) poems that live within a collection but do little for the reader outside of it. This is the issue that Alice must deal with in the collection as a whole, and she has already taken a stand by identifying the project as a collection, rather than individual poems.

Bobbie Troy wrote:
In retrospect, I see that we all should have read the Seven Stages of Man before reading and critiquing Alice's poems. Ain't hindsight great?

Saltian

My approach was that the poem should stand alone and obviously be part of the stage of life that it was meant to represent. The conundrum is that we did not have a chance to glimpse the entire body of work, and therefore, presuming to judge that one poem "fits" within the collection could only be done on a superficial level.

This project is a great learning experience for all of us, and especially for Alice. I admire Alice's courage to do this and hope to hear what tidbits of wisdom she gleans from it. And thanks, Annmarie, for making it happen.

Alice Shapiro

Second Chances

YOUNGER GIRL

In this particular case
much time passed
in solitary confinement
not chained inside a physical prison
parted from the world by bars and guards
but hidden in the corner of an eye
whose depth and breadth of vision
delved far in only one direction—within
like a searchlight on a lonely
lighthouse sandbar
spying distant shipwrecks
searching for a sign of life.

AN OLD GIRL

Like a child develops
to one day see
words appear from single letters,
this old crone was shocked to find
a body connected to her head
not within a physical structure
of sinew and bone
but vibrant in the world of flowers,
hours spent with friends
doing what were once
merely wishful thoughts colliding, parting
staying separate, each alone.

DOWN TO EARTH

It is the glue of mind expanding
ruling who we are
what phase of darkness
it is our time to overcome.

Critique
By Jena Salon

In the first section, "Younger Girl," I love the feeling of yearning and loneliness that's created by what I imagine is a teenager. The way at that time of life we see our own thoughts and imperfections as separations rather than connections. The idea of a searchlight is nice, but I don't quite follow the turn to it looking for distant shipwrecks and seeking survivors. You think more of a lighthouse preventing shipwrecks, so if the searchlight is perched on that same sandbar, I think more of destruction that is so close, and yet you couldn't prevent it, all you can do is look for survivors.

The second section, the emotions are right, and it, too, has a strong opening; but the turn to "friends doing what were once merely wishful thoughts colliding" doesn't make sense to me. The rest of the section is grounded in a way this phrase isn't.

The meaning of the last section is nice and ties the other two sections together in a new way. There seems to be something at odds here—something I believe you mean to exploit more fully —between the title "Down to Earth" which coming after a progression from old to young seems to reference death, and the idea of getting second chances for "overcoming." This could be played up to create more of an arc for the piece—more cohesive with the idea of life—rather than an artificial segmentation.

Failing

Sweated palms holding on
to a ballroom staircase
jerk along a wobbling banister
testament to an old building high-held
once laughter-filled with great music
rising towards a tin-embossed ceiling.

It is a good match to knees
that meet each step with trepidation
anticipating a crumbling destiny.
Distant from a child
whose fearless legs fly
from top stair to bottom.

It is hardly part of one's memory
hardly stored in the cells of bones
now bowed and softened
no cushion for a fall.

I long for the spirit body of health,
of strength, no pain, no disintegration
and aim to live this day as if
I am in heaven.

Critique
By Kenneth Karrer

Sweated palms holding on
to a ballroom staircase

Alice Shapiro

jerk along a wobbling banister
testament to an old building
high-held
once laughter-filled with great music
rising towards a tin-embossed ceiling.   *tin-embossed ceiling, such a perfect detail, it makes the poem and that it appears early on is so much the better*

It is a good match to knees
that meet each step with trepidation
anticipating a crumbling destiny.   *Would you consider "crumbly"?*

Distant from a child
whose fearless legs fly
from top stair to bottom.   *on stairway, top to bottom*

It is hardly part of one's memory   *I don't know if you get much value added from the repetition of "hardly." Could you substitute*

hardly stored in the cells of bones   *"partly of one's memory... hardly stored in the cells of now bowed and softened bones"?*

no cushion for a fall.   *The fall for a fall? Totally different, but just wondered if you considered it.*

Saltian

I long for the spirit body of health,
of strength, no pain, no disintegration
and aim to live this day as if
I am in heaven

Wow, this is nicely done. I have only a few suggestions, mostly related to style and emphasis, and a few thoughts for the poet—a very good poet—to consider. I enjoyed reading this.

An editor friend of mine once told me about her aging grandfather and how one day they came home to find that, after battling Alzheimer's for many years, the old man was in the back yard with a shovel, standing next to a little pile of dirt where he'd buried his favorite felt hat. They decided to put him in a home that day thinking that he'd finally lost it. My comment was that he'd decided to make a final statement, assert some control, and create a memory (ironically) for his family. Then I wrote this poem and gave it to her. I'd forgotten about it until I read "Failing." My thanks to the author for that. I would say that "Failing" is the perfect piece to end the Pantaloon section.

Responsive Writing
To Grandpa, who beat the hell out of Alzheimer's
(I finally figured out why you planted your felt hat in our back yard.)
By Kenneth Karrer

I wonder still at how
It could catch up
To you.

Alice Shapiro

You always took such
Giant steps
And yet its shuffling
Overtook your gait

Your absolute lucidity
Fell at last it seemed to a
Stumbling, slurred, then quiet fate.

But what I hated most
Was how it
Wrapped,
Entwined,
And seemed to squeeze the
Brightness
From your mind.

It was as if it took you
Down
A hole
Into
A den
And to a place from which
They said, "He won't come back again."

And in the end it was not with
Suicide,
Or rage,
Or resignation
That you fought back

Saltian

You stood your ground
(And in point of fact dug in)
With simple
Dignity
And sense that was
Uncommon
In the face of such insidious attack.

And I'll always think of you and smile
When I look back
And
See the memories that play
Around the place
Where
You planted your favorite felt hat
In our back yard
That day.

Alice Shapiro

Moving on

Bring on the aphorisms
the diet pills
drape the mirror darkly, in chiffon
to hide a glimpse of aging skin
lusterless, droopy eyes
double chin.

In youth the flesh is weak
near death it's loose
on shrinking bones,
a gradual warning
meant to ease transition
from faulty flesh to spirit zones.

Oldness is cold to the clinging eye
but warm, knowing that upon selection
one is soon to meet
the Holy Presence
and soon to be
breathing young again.

Carey High School bleachers

Having descended an inch
from a previous height
to view the football field
eyes must peer atop
a hoard of spectators' spectacles
to have the widest view ...

Saltian

From bleachers, a grandchild's grandeur
gets blurred and embittered
by the nonsense of age.

From this oligarchic perch
the old woman
distracted from quarterback, cheerleaders,
pomp and circumstance
follows the hawk up, up.
While a crowd's roar fades away
she sniffs the joy of new grass
goes back into the cocoon of
faraway youth

coddles her
coddles everyone's
ageless spirit.

Critique: Responsive Writing
Response From a Thirty-Something
By Julie Ellinger Hunt

Glued to solid ground,
I envy the turning aged
from seedling to tree,
to even the falling, wasted wood
where life is somewhat figured
out and not floating with
uncertainties.

Alice Shapiro

In between the new day's frost
and lunar eclipse,
I hold onto the finest edge
and walk the proverbial
tightrope toward inner peace.
Years can stack up behind me.
I welcome them.

Anything is better than this ...

Responsive Art
Salient Love
By Julie Ellinger Hunt

Hell's kitchen

His accent reeks New York
that high-energy island
where a daily frenzied pace can kill
soot collects on window sills
sharing nostrils with seductive cocaine crack.

Biology catches up, eventually,
and faded body paint
branded into forearms
extracts metallic pain
when wheeled into an MRI machine.

He takes to bed to rest and cower
most unlike his youthful zeal
when sheets and pillows were wildly scattered
onto a city floor
as he explored a lover's bower.

Critique
By Andrew Badger

Of all Alice's poems that I've read, "Hell's kitchen" is her strongest. Her imagery and diction create both hell and death, supporting her male protagonist. Her poetic rhythms move smoothly through most of the poem. However, there are two places where the diction is wrong, and there are three places where her diction misses both the male protagonist and the Hell established at the very beginning. My suggestions are intended to make a strong poem even stronger.

Alice Shapiro

First, the two places where I believe the diction is wrong. The title of the poem, Hell's kitchen, works well with Hell, but the poem misses everything that "kitchen" denotes or could possibly connote. I think the title could enhance the poem more if it focused on either the protagonist—such as denizen, or on the setting—possibly flophouse. But the only place we see "kitchen" is in the title. Next, the last line of stanza 1 ends with crack cocaine. According to my most reliable druggie friend, crack would not share the nostrils with soot. But just soot and seductive cocaine could really share a good snort.

Second, the three places where the diction allows us to avoid both Hell and maleness. The second stanza opens with a pop—biology—when it could deliver a bang. The entire first line dozes when it should crackle. I'd suggest the line to read "Abuse eventually exacts its dues" and change the "and" in the next line to "even." The final line of the stanza, "wheeled into an MRI machine," again allows the reader to doze. My most reliable medical friend (not the druggie), told me that one of the most intimidating aspects of an MRI was the constant pulsing of the machine. Thus, I'd suggest rewriting the line as "when dragged through a pulsing MRI." And finally, in the third stanza, "as he explored a lover's bower" evokes Venus and possibly paradise, not a Hell-bound male. Furthermore, a second end rhyme in the poem (kill/sills in stanza 1) seems out of place in an unrhymed poem. Again, I have an alternative: replace "as he explored a lover's bower" with "entwined lovers' passions." Perhaps a little more Mars than Venus, but I don't think it evokes Hell.

Now to follow precedent rather than our instructions, I'll include a fourth paragraph—my emendations of Alice's poem:

Saltian

Hell's denizen

His accent reeks New York
that high-energy island
where a daily frenzied pace can kill
soot collects on window sills
sharing nostrils with seductive cocaine.

Abuse eventually exacts its dues,
even faded body paint
branded into forearms
extracts metallic pain
when dragged through a pulsing MRI.

He takes to bed to rest and cower
most unlike his youthful zeal
when sheets and pillows wildly scattered
on a city floor
entwined lovers' passions.

My suggestions are made without seeing this poem in context.

Reader comments

Joan McNerney wrote:
I think this poem is very strong but untrue. It furthers the myth that all New Yorkers are drug addicts. Having lived outside and inside the great city, I can tell you New Yorkers work hard and play hard, but have lower crime rates than the rest of the country. I did, however, find the poem to be very compelling. Too bad it was not about an accident or illness rather than drugs.

Alice Shapiro

The strength of old ideals

The pain, the pain
the pain, the pain
the pain
of eighty-eight

is calmed
only by such meditations I can muster
as the tale of fishermen I see
from my summer balcony.

The ramblings of my day's events
prevents her body's
dwelling on
monstrous unpleasantness.

I wonder when her tolerance will fade
and a crackling exhortation to the Lord
burst out her drawn shut mouth?
I have seen lesser men succumb.

Critique
By Stan Galloway

I like the way that the poem begins with the pulsing repetition of "the pain." At first it might seem gimmicky, but the transition of the last line of the first stanza brings a balance and a context that I think works. At first, the "I" of stanza 2 and the "her" of stanza 3 is confusing, but I think it sorts out with the realization that the speaker is interacting with the older character rather than the older character being the narrator. The realization that there are 2 characters adds a desirable complexity to the poem. Now we have the sufferer and the meditator/mediator for the older woman. The younger person provides essential distraction for the 88-year-old by telling her about her day, neatly captured in "The ramblings of my day's events," and "the tale of fishermen I see/from my summer balcony," (the only rhyme of the poem, but a fitting one at the midpoint, because it isn't predicted, yet provides a sense of completion to the first half of the poem).

The second half of the poem shows the resolve of the older woman, which is not hinted at in the first half. The "monstrous unpleasantness" is ambiguous, euphemistic, and poignant all at once, because most readers will find anything "monstrous" undesirable, but it's not pain here, or injustice, or any earth-shaking trauma; it's simple understated "unpleasantness." The last stanza moves from the condition to the speculation of the younger character. The older woman's Job-like resolve is admired by the speaker and the reference to the Lord makes the situation cosmic rather than temporal. The reader will wonder whether the mouth "drawn shut" is a medical condition or a spiritual one, but the answer is moot. The woman will not complain about her situation. And it is this resolve that illuminates the final line. It is probably no accident that the final line invokes gender separations, though noticing that is not essential. This woman outlasts men her age because of her "old ideal" invoked in the title to not charge any deity with unfairness but to suffer in silence.

Alice Shapiro

Circles

She's ninety-two
and sad to say
discredits every knock
and friendship
at the door.

She's sure, as if
still six in years
loving her kaleidoscopic eyes
in pretty mirrors
that hate won't harm.

All reality out of proportion
backwards
like her view
untouched by Death's immanence
she demands perfection.

It is I who sees
the judgment
my eye discerning
discontent, the hurt
that her old heart embraces

and I forbid myself
this poor future
announce to you
such foolish trend
so that if and when I reach

her long-lived end
at least you will have heard of
frailty
and might forgive an aged parent's
petty flaw.

Critique
By David B Axelrod

My mother   *by starting with "my" I am prepared for the shift to "I" below*

is ninety-two
and discredits
every knock
and friendship
at the door.

When young
it was loving,
kaleidoscopic eyes   *I'm setting up a "then/now" thing with little adjustments to make it flow*

in pretty mirrors
that hate could
not harm.

Now, death's
immanence
demands perfection
and she can't see
the hurt her old
heart embraces.

Alice Shapiro

I forbid myself
this future, or
so intend, but
if I reach her
long-lived end   *This is a doubly good ending as it gives and*
                    asks forgiveness!
forgive an aged   *I speeded it up a bit to make it end more*
                    dramatically
parent's petty flaw.

A lovely poem! Hooray for Alice!

Saltian

Randomness near the end

a.

If not for spaces between one chaos and another
would I lose a grip
on love, on peace
on knowing when to bring
the trash to curb on Sunday eve?

b.

A late sun empties its dwindling warmth
on my shoulder
so I may drench my soul with the heat
my belief with hope
my gratitude with the inner smile
of one who knows the undeserved sometimes reap
what others sow
       a life of toil, wrong attitudes
          unproductive moves, unrelenting descents
          into oblivion must be sent packing.

c.

From a perch on a bent tree
dangling on a fragile bench
wondering if a leap will bring a fall
or flight into another wondrous conquest,
eyes close, ablaze.

Alice Shapiro

Critique
By Courtney Leigh Jameson

The first two stanzas seem somewhat abstract with the use of words like "hope," "love," "peace"—those are very obscure and more emotional, not physical. It would be nice to replace these words maybe with some physical representation of peace, love, or hope. The last stanza has detailed images where I can physically see the "conquest" taking place. The first two stanzas are also a bit wordy and could use a reduction. For instance, "on my shoulder,/drenching me in the heat/like hope shown through/my inner smile ... " That would encompass the physical embodiment of hope, "through the inner smile" and cut down on some of the random language. The idea of the poem is interesting though because these are random things at the end ... the end being a different outcome for each stanza, each image. And the "undeserved reap" is a great image/line!

Here and hereafter

At times past sixty
glimpses of the human's exit
from body-bound blessedness
strike a sudden chord
start me wondering
and I go somewhere inexplicable
just an instant.

I expect to pile these keepsakes one upon another
more and more
until acceptance becomes a picture formed
like a mason builds a house
decorated and cluttered
that throws wide its doors
invites me in, commands a fine
free flight.

Critique
By Gloria Mindock

Looking at one's own mortality is not an easy thing to do. This poem addresses this issue in so few lines. I love the preciseness of the language. It is straight to the point. It also speaks about one of my favorite topics, death. Alice's poem has a beautiful sadness to it. The poem makes me think, since I'm older, I should get my things in order. She has a way with words that many writers could learn from.

In the first stanza, I would cut the line, "from body-bound blessedness." I think it is a much stronger stanza with this line cut out. Therefore it would read: "glimpses of the human's exit/ strike a sudden chord." This makes the flow in the first stanza so much better.

In the second stanza, I would cut the second line "more & more." You already said the same thing in the first line of the poem, "I expect to pile these keepsakes one upon another."

Having read other poetry by Alice, I can't wait to read this book! This is an exciting project and I am so excited to be a part of it.

Reader comments

Rae Spencer wrote:
I love Gloria Mindock's description of this poem as possessing "a beautiful sadness." I agree with the suggested line deletions, and would further recommend deleting the final line of the first stanza, "just an instant."

The last stanza, particularly the last two lines, lost me. Keepsakes assembling into a picture is a lovely way to describe life, but the picture metaphor gets lost in the transition to building a house and then on to "...a fine/free flight." I prefer the picture metaphor, though the house metaphor is clear and meaningful. Progressing into flight lost me.

Perhaps the final phrase isn't necessary? Slight adjustments to word order would yield, "... decorated and cluttered/doors thrown wide/in invitation." (There are many possible variations for this. My point is to avoid moving away from the house metaphor.)

Saltian

Carlene Tejada wrote:
I agree with Gloria's praise for Alice's poems and her suggestions for deletions. I would go further and delete "decorated and cluttered." I prefer going from the mason building the house to entering the front door. The "decorated and cluttered" line seems misplaced.

Alice Shapiro

Saltian

Old English word meaning "to dance"

*

Eyes of sixty-five
remember lessons
clearer than a school child.
Old clumps of pain-visions accumulate
outdated and worn like a 45
vinyl song
along with joyful thoughts
peaks and valleys, strong
photo'd footholds from the past.

*

The ear of eighty
folds in on itself
as present sounds and conversations lapse.
A hidden chamber filled with wet dreams
rises to the top.
Lost senses brew again
from that squirreled-away
often nasty, occasionally happy
cache.

*

Not ripe enough
to leap and twirl
our mind still dances
as milk-white bones of ninety—

porous, brittle, bent
these rounded immanent fossils—
dip towards earth
until they shed the law
and their temporary birth.

*

Freed from dirt-encumbered form
a light-body, as at its young peak
travels easy
eats the fruit of health, well-being, truth
its spirit-heart an everlasting melody
uncontaminated by Sin
and evil
blotted out
like acrid smoke rising from the spit.

Critique
By Laura C Lieberman

Replete with hyphenates, Shapiro's language in her collection's title poem recalls the lucid poetics of Old English's simple compounds—and refers to the status (if not the melancholy spirit) of Shakespeare's seven stages of man, addressed by Jaques in Act II, Scene vii, of *As You Like It*. However, not too much can or should be made of Shapiro's Shakespearean reference; her starting point is the Dance—of life, and of death, closer to the idea of medieval theatre's spectacles of the *danse macabre* (led by a personified Death figure, absent in this poem) reminding audiences of the universality of mortality, whatever status one may have had in life.

Alice Shapiro

In Shapiro's dance, at last at death we are freed from our mortal coil, lifted sinless and refined into pure spirit. Her previous stanzas describe the encumbrances of our worn bodies and personal histories—pain and pleasure of memories in our sixties, failing senses and lost passions in our eighties, and the fragility and bone loss in our nineties. One wonders a bit if the seventies are skipped over simply because they have not been imagined, or if the poet's decade-ism just needs a bit more development.

Within all the swirling, rising force of her poem, Shapiro has offered some vivid poetic images ("blotted out like acrid smoke rising from the spit," "rounded immanent fossils —/dip towards earth," "The ear of eighty/folds in on itself," and even "photo'd footholds"), along with some clunkers that could use better resolution (especially in the final stanza's "happily ever after" mode where we could use some eloquent, elegiac convincing —"its spirit-heart an everlasting melody" and "that squirreled-away/often nasty, occasionally happy/cache," the "occasionally" seems an especially awkward adverb there but the whole phrase needs reconsideration.

One word in Anglo Saxon, Old English for soul or spirit is *gast* (literally "breath"), and *gastgiefu* means "a gift of the holy spirit" (literally translated as "breath gift"), often interpreted as a "gift of tongues." Another charming construction is the word *ellorsip*, or "journey elsewhere," referring to the departures of death. I am especially fond of the following explication of the word: *eftforgiefnes* (strong feminine noun) "a sending back or away, releasing, a sending back, returning of persons or things, a throwing back, reflecting, a letting down, lowering, a slackening, relaxing, abating, diminishing, remitting, remission, relaxation, abatement, slackness, laxness, want of spirit, relaxation, recreation, mildness, gentleness, lenity, a remitting of a penalty etc, a remission, *in eccl. lat.*, remission, forgiveness of sin, a repetition, a re-establishing, reinstatement, restoration, renewal," literally put a renewed or "second forgiveness."

Alice Shapiro

A-head

Beating footprints on concrete
leaves marks and shadows if we turn to look.
The neck, curious as Lot's wife
commands reversal
and possible blockage to a pleasant walk.
The head, that fragile instrument of peace and evil
guides and reasons, soothes, abuses
invests, invites, deletes.
Mine in particular is king
or queen subordinating limbs
and organs, feet
do its bidding.

I am my head.
It is sometimes red and wrathful
green and cool
it takes me where it wants to
an everlasting tool
like driver's education school.
I cannot turn it off
even if it acts The Fool.
I plan to take it with me
in its spirit body
when a head no longer rules
this solitary earthly journey.

Critique
By Annmarie Lockhart

I had the great honor of publishing Alice Shapiro's "A-head" at *vox poetica* as part of Contributor Series 5: Dramatis Personae, a series that explored identity. I've come to think of "A-head" as the first poem in this collection, a collection that also explores identity, using the template laid down by Shakespeare and deftly lifting the corners of curtains to give us a glimpse into those hidden spaces where the self dances in the dark before no perceived audience. It's a messy room, piles of stripped-off clothes on the floor, books scattered across the bed, sheets rumpled and lumped, cosmetic spills in sticky splotches in front of the mirror, shoes kicked off and tripped over from bed to door. Don't we recognize not only the dwelling of our personae, but the various poses practiced in this habitation as well?

Alice's poem, employing imagery from the Bible to the Bard, invites us to play peek-a-boo with her identity and our own. She warns us to leave our vanity at the door and to brace for untapped potential instead of profound accomplishment. Her tone, while unflinching, is also affectionate and playful (see the rhyme sequence in stanza 2), and this is what endears the reader to the work, the unseen audience to the dancer, the introspective self to the exhibitionist personalities pirouetting around the room. The first stanza invites us to examine our own "footprints over concrete," an image suggestive at once of sidewalk artwork and time-worn crumbles, and to risk seeing what we do not wish to see. She identifies us with Lot's wife and paints our need to witness as the great self-imposed impediment to happiness.

The second stanza ties the narrator (and by extension, the reader) to the fallible "head," capricious as it may be: "It's sometimes red and wrathful/green and cool" and Alice goes on to decree: "I cannot turn it off/even if it acts The Fool." This is the crux upon which the poem, and also *Saltian* the book, seems

Alice Shapiro

to balance: we are who we are, study it, ignore it, dress it up or play it down, but we are still, in the end, stuck with it. This can be a frightening prospect when one considers the darker elements Alice hints at and explores to a greater degree in the book, but the genius of the poem lies in the redemption found in its final four lines: "I plan to take it with me/in its spirit body/when a head no longer rules/this solitary earthly journey." And what a redemption it is, speaking of transformation, legacy, and spirituality while steering clear of dogma, creed, and faith. I would not change a thing in this poem.

This declared acceptance of self, with all its inherent flaws and faults, has been integral to this work-in-progress. Not every writer would open herself to wholesale commentary and critique. Alice Shapiro has offered her words to public scrutiny with openness and grace. As we embark on the next phase of production Alice will be reconsidering each of these poems in the light of the suggestions seen here. I don't have any idea what the final poems will look like; I suspect Alice doesn't either. But I do know this work has been dynamic and energetic and alive and once again, I am honored to be a part of its publication.

Editorial Board

Dr. **David B Axelrod** is an author and sponsor of international writers' programs covering dozens of countries and nearly 40 languages. He has presented as an author and educator globally. Dr. Axelrod is a student of 10 languages and author of 19 books and hundreds of articles. He is the only American to receive 2 back-to-back Fulbright Awards in separate areas (poet-in-residence in Yugoslavia and professor of American literature in Macedonia). With the award of his third Fulbright he became the first poet to be formally acknowledged as American Poet-in-Residence in the People's Republic of China. Dr. Axelrod is the founder and vice president for Florida programs of Writers Unlimited Agency and he is founder and director of Creative Happiness Institute, Inc. For more information, visit his website, PoetryDoctor.org.

Andrew Badger is a writer and poet (and retired professor—Delta State University) whose work has appeared in *Magnolia Quarterly* and whose academic papers have appeared in numerous journals. His poem "Shaving Dad" won 1st place in the Picayune Writer's Group annual contest in 2010. His chapbook *Out on a Limb* was released earlier in 2011.

Maxwell Baumbach is a manchild from Elmhurst IL. He is the editor of *Heavy Hands Ink*. He has authored the chapbooks *Suburban Rhythm* (Scars Publications, September 2010) and *You're Welcome* (Alternating Current, March 2011). His first full-length collection, *At Age Twenty*, is slated for a spring 2012 release from unbound CONTENT. In his spare time, Maxwell enjoys watching unhealthy amounts of Sports Center and sleeping.

Alice Shapiro

Bryan Borland is a Pushcart-nominated poet from Little Rock AR and the owner of Sibling Rivalry Press. His first book, *My Life as Adam*, was 1 of only 5 collections of poetry included on the American Library Association's Over the Rainbow list of notable LGBT-themed books published in 2010. He is the founding editor of *Assaracus*, the only print journal in the world dedicated exclusively to the poetry of gay men. His work has appeared in *Gay & Lesbian Review Worldwide, Breadcrumb Scabs, Referential Magazine, vox poetica, Ganymede,* and *Velvet Mafia,* among others.

KC Bosch lives and writes in Virginia, and this place appears as a character in his writing as frequently as people do. His craft, be it wordworking or woodworking, is what he spends his time on and he takes his inspiration from both interior and exterior landscapes. You can read his words at *vox poetica, Camel Saloon,* and *Poetry Breakfast.*

Charles Clifford Brooks III has had work published in *The Dead Mule, Eclectica, Gloom Cupboard, The Smoking Poet, Red Fez, vox poetica, Asylum, Alba, Prick of the Spindle, Zygote in My Coffee,* and *The Cartier Street Review.* His poetry has been featured on the Joe Milford Poetry Show and *vox poetica's* 15 Minutes of Poetry. Charles' first book of poetry, *Whirling Metaphysics,* is in the final stages of production at Gosslee with an imminent release date.

Ray Brown began writing in 1987 in the midst of a personal crisis. For the next 20 years he wrote on the back of napkins, on reports in business meetings, on index cards, in a small notebook, on his computer. In December 2008, he started his blog, Poetry by Ray Brown. Ray's work has been published at journals including *The*

Edison Literary Review, The Blue Collar Review, FreeXpresSion, The River Poets Journal, The New Jersey Poetry Society Anthology, Big Hammer, The River, and *vox poetica*. His first collection of poetry, *I Have His Letters Still,* is available at Amazon. A graduate of the University of Notre Dame, Ray returned to his alma mater to hold a poetry reading at his 40th reunion. He lives and writes in Frenchtown NJ.

Grace Burns lives in New Jersey with her husband and 2 children. She is an engineer, a wedding DJ and an aspiring creative writer. Her poems have appeared at *vox poetica* and SPARK and have also been included in a number of *vox poetica* print anthologies.

Joanie DiMartino has work published in many literary journals and anthologies. Her first chapbook, *Licking the Spoon,* was published with Finishing Line Press in 2007. She is a past winner of the Betty Gabehart Award for poetry from the Women Writers Conference, Kentucky, and was a finalist in the Cultural Center of Cape Cod poetry competition. Her first full-length collection, *Strange Girls,* was published in June 2010 by Little Red Tree Publishing, and the poem "A Treatise on Handling Snakes" from that collection has received a nomination for a Pushcart Prize. *Strange Girls* has been nominated for the 2011 Connecticut Book Award.

Walter Elmore is a recent graduate of the University of West Georgia who is looking for an opportunity to showcase his editorial skills for a publishing group, newspaper, or magazine. He has worked as a copy editor and fact checker for the past several years.

Sarah Endo lives in Massachusetts with her family. Her poems have been published online at *vox poetica* and *Literary Mama,* and in unbound CONTENT anthologies.

Stan Galloway teaches writing and literature at Bridgewater College in the Shenandoah Valley of Virginia. His poetry has appeared online and in print at journals including *vox poetica, Loch Raven Review, Indigo Rising Magazine, Eunoia Review, Contemporary World Literature, Assisi: An Online Journal of Arts and Letters, Apollo's Lyre, WestWard Quarterly,* and *the Burroughs Bulletin,* and the anthologies *Love Be Write* and *Edgar Rice Burroughs: The Second Century.* His book of literary criticism, *The Teenage Tarzan,* came out in 2010.

John Gosslee is the editor of *Fjords Arts and Literary Review,* a twice yearly national magazine with first-ever audio-only selections. He is also the founder of Gosslee, a new traditional press.

Robert C J Graves' poetry and fiction are widely published in print and online, including recent publications in *Poetry Quarterly, vox poetica, Fear and Trembling Magazine, Danse Macabre, Leaf Garden,* and *Clockwise Cat.* He lives in Augusta, GA, where he is a Professor of English at Paine College.

KJ Hannah Greenberg gave up all manner of academic hoopla to chase imaginary hedgehogs and to raise children. After almost 2 decades of belly dancing, home birthing, herbal medicine making and occasional basket weaving, she dusted off her keyboard and began to churn out smoothies, vegetable soup, and more creative work than might be considered proper for a middle-aged woman. Hannah formed Expressedly Yours Writing Workshops, took on editorial responsibilities at publications hither and yon, and was nominated for a Pushcart Prize. She established a matchmaking service for words such as "twaddle" and "xylophone," too. Incorrigible to a molecular level, Hannah continues to write across genres. Look for her blogs and columns in publications including

Israel's *The Jerusalem Post* and the UK's *The Mother Magazine*. Enjoy her fiction in print and in electronic broadcasts in forums ranging from *Bewildering Stories, Morpheus Tales,* and *Weirdyear* to *Bartleby Snopes, MENSA's Calliope, Fallopian Falafel,* and *The Journal of Microliterature*. Consider buying Hannah's other books, the latest poetry collection *A Bank Robber's Bad Luck With His Ex-Girlfriend*, the collection of light essays, *Oblivious to the Obvious: Wishfully Mindful Parenting,* the scholarly *Conversations on Communication Ethics,* and the just released, *Don't Pet the Sweaty Things*.

Julie Ellinger Hunt lives in Northwest New Jersey. After completing her education at the University of Delaware, Hunt published her poetry in more than 20 journals internationally. Her off-beat, gritty style fused with sentiment and surreal observation is well received by the literary community. Her first book, *Ever Changing* (Publish America, 2010), was well regarded by fellow writers and happy readers. Her second book of poetry, *In New Jersey*, was released in 2011 by unbound CONTENT and it is rising up the Amazon charts with a fury. She hopes to continue to grow as a writer and contribute as much as possible while living under the same roof with her 2 sons and husband (she speculates they may be part alien). Keep up with her at http://jthunt.wordpress.com/.

Courtney Leigh Jameson is the Editor in Chief of The Bruised Peach Press poetry zine, a monthly newsletter dedicated to people who have a passion for poetry. She received her Bachelor of Arts in Creative Writing at Arizona State University and is currently attending Saint Mary's College of California for her MFA in poetry.

Alice Shapiro

Ashok Karra blogs at http://www.ashokkarra.com. He studies political science and enjoys poetry, disciplines that have more in common than people think. You can read about what he's trying to achieve in some of his interviews. A sample of how poetry and political science might converge can be seen in Lincoln's rhetoric, which requires careful attention to words to unpack: Abraham Lincoln, "Proclamation of Thanksgiving."

Kenneth Karrer grew up just outside Austin, Texas hauling hay, working on oil rigs, pumping gas, and playing football. He received degrees in English, history, and education and worked as a teacher, coach, and high school administrator for 32 years. Ken lives in Austin and now works for the Texas Education Agency. He is a musician and an avid car restorer. His poems have recently been featured in *vox poetica* and *Caper Literary Journal*.

Joanna S Lee lives in Richmond VA where she spends her free time searching the riverbanks for unborn poetry. Her first book, *the somersaults I did as I fell*, was released in 2009. Her work has been recently featured at *Catapult to Mars, Bolts of Silk,* and *vox poetica*. She writes (semi-)regularly at the Tenth Muse.

Laura C Lieberman is Executive Director of the Cultural Arts Council of Douglasville/Douglas County, Inc.

Annmarie Lockhart is the founding editor of *vox poetica* (an online literary salon dedicated to bringing poetry into the every day) and unbound CONTENT (an independent press for a boundless age).

Saltian

Her own poetry has been published at fine journals in print and online. A lifelong resident of Bergen County NJ, she lives 2 miles east of the hospital where she was born.

Leah Maines has served as senior editor for Finishing Line Press since she took over in 2002. She has edited more than 600 poetry collections, including several award-winning titles. She is former Poet-in-Residence of Northern Kentucky University (funded in part by the Kentucky Humanities Council and the National Endowment for the Humanities). Her first book was nominated for the Pushcart Prize and the William Carlos Williams Book Award (Poetry Society of America). *Looking to the East with Western Eyes*, New Women's Voices Series, No. 1 (Finishing Line Press, 1998) reached #10 in the "Cincinnati/Tri-State Best Sellers List" (Cincinnati Enquirer) and is now in its fourth printing. Her most recent collection, *Beyond the River*, (KWC Press, 2002, 1st edition) won the Kentucky Writers' Coalition Poetry Chapbook Competition in 2002. Her poems have appeared in numerous national and international publications including *Nebo, Owen Wister Review, Licking River Review,* and *Flyway*. Maines studied and researched classical Japanese poetry at Gifu University in Gifu, Japan. She also studied at Kings College London, England and The Marino Institute in Dublin, Ireland. She lives with her husband and children in Central Kentucky.

Jean McLeod is a sometimes poet, full-time joyful person, happy beach bum, and fortunate friend of talented writers. Her recent work has appeared at journals such as *vox poetica, Leaf Garden Press, Word Gathering, Spinetinglers, Rust+Moth,* and *Touch: the Journal of Healing*.

Kay Middleton is a member of the Albright Poets, a group to which she was accepted after writing the obligatory limerick. In addition to poetry she writes flash, shorts, and historical fiction. She has been rejected by some of the finest publications on the planet and accepted by others. Publication credits include *vox poetica*, *Eat a Peach*, *Concise Delights*, *Lines & Stars*, *Rust + Moth*, *Punkin House Digest*, *Leaf Garden Press*, *Bolts of Silk*, and *Contemporary American Voices*. Nominated for the 2011 Pushcart Prize, she has work forthcoming at *Right Hand Pointing*. You can read and hear more of her work at her website: kaymiddleton.net.

Gloria Mindock is the editor of Červená Barva Press and the *Istanbul Literary Review*. She is the author of *Nothing Divine Here* (U Soku Stampa, Montenegro, 2010), *La Portile Raiului* (Ars Longa Press, Romania, 2010, translated into the Romanian by Flavia Cosma), and *Blood Soaked Dresses* (Ibbetson St. Press, 2007). Her work has been published in numerous literary journals in the United States and abroad and translated into Spanish, Romanian, and French. For more information, visit: www.cervenabarvapress.com.

Hans Ostrom's recent books include *The Coast Starlight: Collected Poems, 1976-2006* and *Honoring Juanita*, a novel. He co-edited *The Greenwood Encyclopedia of African American Literature*. His YouTube channel, langstonify, features recordings of poetry.

Born in Greenwood SC, **Scott Owens** lives in Hickory NC, where he coordinates the Poetry Hickory reading series and Writers' Night Out, edits *Wild Goose Poetry Review* and *234*, and writes the weekly poetry column "Musings in Outlook." He is regional representative for the North Carolina Writers' Network and vice president of the Poetry Council of North Carolina. He holds degrees from Ohio University, UNC-Charlotte, and UNC-Greensboro and teaches English and creative writing at Catawba Valley Community College. Scott is the author of *Something Knows the Moment* (Main Street Rag, August 2011), *Paternity* (Main Street Rag, 2010), *The Fractured World* (Main Street Rag, 2008), and 3 chapbooks. More than 800 of his poems have been published in literary journals. His work has received awards from the Academy of American Poets, the Pushcart Press, the NC Writers' Network, the NC Poetry Society, and the Poetry Society of SC, has been nominated for 7 Pushcart Prizes and 7 Best of the Net awards, and has been read by Garrison Keillor on *The Writer's Almanac*.

Jena Salon is the books editor of The Literary Review. Her essays and reviews have appeared or are forthcoming *inn+1, Bookforum*, and *The Collagist*.

Ray Sharp writes poems inspired by the wooded hills of the rural, rugged and remote Michigan Western Upper Peninsula region. He knew he wanted to be a writer when he read Ken Kesey's *Sometimes a Great Notion* during a wet and miserable winter in Oregon; he discovered poetry reading Federico Garcia Lorca's *Bodas de sangre* while earning a BA in Spanish at the University of Colorado. Ray juxtaposes details of the natural world and personal narratives with interior monologues that transcend the textural surfaces to expose the raw human qualities that lie beneath. His poems have been featured at *vox poetica, Caper Journal, Eclectic Flash, Spark, qarrtsiluni,* and *Astropoetica*. He posts new work raysharp.wordpress.com.

Alice Shapiro

Rae Spencer is a writer and veterinarian living in Virginia. Her poetry has been published online and in print, receiving Pushcart Prize nominations in 2009 and 2010. She can be found on the web at www.raespencer.com.

Harrison Solow has received many awards for her literary fiction, nonfiction, cross-genre writing, poetry, and professional writing, most notably winning the Pushcart Prize in 2008. She is one of the two best-selling University of California Press authors of all time (at time of publication) and a notable alumna of Mills College, where she earned her MFA and of the University of Wales where she earned her PhD in English Letters. She lectures at universities, colleges, arts and cultural institutions in the United States, Canada and Great Britain. A former faculty member at UC Berkeley, she accepted a lectureship in the English Department of the University of Wales in 2004 and was appointed Writer in Residence in 2008. She returned to America for 2009-2011 to write her third and fourth books and her PhD dissertation. She lives in the United States and Wales with her husband, Herbert F. Solow, the former Head of MGM, Paramount and Desilu Studios in Hollywood. She has two sons. Her latest book is *Felicity & Barbara Pym*, a genre-defying book about reading, writing, the love of literature and incidentally, Barbara Pym.

After divorce and empty nest, **Carlene Tejada** faced the future armed with an MA in English literature, a BA in teaching English as a second language, and years of editing and teaching experience. Only then did she feel she had the time and focus to take her lifelong fascination with writing seriously. More than anything, she wanted a body of work. Carlene moved many times but always found writing groups. For several years she led journal-writing workshops (and still does). She experimented with short stories, and in drafting a novel she discovered a lack of patience and imagination for writing fiction. At friends' suggestions, she read works by several contemporary poets and was drawn to writing poetry. Poems became the body of work she was working for. *Blue Pearls: Poems* came out in 2010; she is now working on poems for a second book.

Lynne Thompson won the Perugia Press Book Prize for her first full-length collection of poems, *Beg No Pardon*, which was also awarded the Great Lakes Colleges Association New Writers Award. Thompson also coauthored 2 poetry chapbooks: *We Arrive By Accumulation* and *Through a Window*. Her work has appeared in numerous journals and anthologies including *Sou'wester, Indiana Review, Spillway, Ploughshares,* and *New Poets of the American West*. A 2010 recipient of a fellowship from the SLS Summer Literary Seminars, she is the director of employee and labor relations at the University of California, Los Angeles.

Bobbie Troy maintains her sanity and perspective on life by writing flash fiction, poetry, and original fairy tales with a 21st century twist. Her work appears online and in print at *Concise Delights Magazine of Short Poetry, Issue 1; vox poetica* website and anthologies; *SPARK*, an art and writing project; *Haiku Ramblings; Caper Literary Journal; Leaf Garden Press; the Journal of Liberal Arts and Education; Referential Magazine; Yes, Poetry; Cavalcade of Stars; The Journal of Microliterature*. Her poem "Dear Diane "was nominated for a 2010 Pushcart Prize (www.aliceshapiro.com/thechangeinterviews.html). Her fairy tale play "Sasha and the Tree of Sorrows" was produced in March 2011.

Jim Valvis lives in Issaquah WA. His poems and short stories have recently appeared in *Arts & Letters, Front Porch Journal, LA Review, Pank, River Styx,* and *Verdad* and he has work forthcoming at journals including *Clackamas Literary Review, Hanging Loose, GW Review, New York Quarterly,* and *Slipstream*. His fiction has been named a *storySouth* Notable Story twice and his poetry has been nominated for Pushcart and Best of the Web anthologies numerous times. His full-length poetry collection *How to Say Goodbye* is available now.

Bill Yarrow is Professor of English at Joliet Junior College where he teaches literature, film, and creative writing online. He is the author of *WRENCH* (erbacce-press, 2009) and *Wound Jewelry* (new aesthetic, 2010). His poems have appeared in many print and online magazines including *Poetry International, Confrontation, Rio Grande Review, Ramshackle Review, Istanbul Literary Review, BLIP, PANK, DIAGRAM, Pif Magazine, Now Culture, Right Hand Pointing, Whale Sounds,* and *Metazen*. More information can be found at his website: livepage.apple.comwww.billyarrow.com.

Alice Shapiro is currently serving as Poet Laureate of Douglasville, GA. Her first collection of poems, *Cracked: Timeless Topics of Nature, Courage, and Endurance* (Total Recall Press 2009), earned her a Pushcart Prize nomination and Georgia Author of the Year nomination (2010). Her second collection, *Life, Descending/Ascending*, also published by Total Recall Press, was released in 2010 to critical acclaim and her one-act play Four Voices won the Bill C. Davis Drama Award for a verse play and was performed as part of the first annual Turner Cassity Literary Festival, July 2011. Alice is Executive Producer of a TV competition for poets, and was one of the judges for Poetry Out Loud's 2010 and 2011 regionals. She serves on the planning board for the Turner Cassity Literary Festival.

Also by Alice Shapiro

Poetry:
Cracked: Timeless Topics of Nature, Courage and Endurance
Life: Descending/Ascending
Play:
Four Voices: A One-Act Play

www.ingramcontent.com/pod-product-compliance
Lightning Source LLC
Chambersburg PA
CBHW071653090426
42738CB00009B/1506